WHY PÍSEK?

MY UNEXPECTED JOURNEY

Cindy Wiese

:: Published by Cynthia E. Wiese ::

Copyright © 2021 Cynthia E. Wiese

All rights reserved.

The events in this book are my memories from my perspective.

C.S. Lewis quotes: © copyright CS Lewis Pte Ltd, used with permission.

Tolkien quotes: every effort has been made to obtain permission from the copyright holder. In the event that the copyright holder wishes to contact me, I would be glad to hear from them.

Unless otherwise indicated, all Scripture quotations are from The ESV ® Bible (The Holy Bible, English Standard Version ®), copyright © 2001 by Crossway, a publishing ministry of Good News Publishers. Used by permission. All rights reserved.

Scripture marked "AMP" taken from THE AMPLIFIED BIBLE, Old Testament copyright © 1965, 1987 by the Zondervan Corporation. Used by permission.

Scripture marked "ERV" taken from the HOLY BIBLE: EASY-TO-READ VERSION © 2001 by World Bible Translation Center, Inc. and used by permission.

Scripture marked "TNIV" taken from the Holy Bible, Today's New International Version ™ TNIV ® Copyright © 2001, 2005 by International Bible Society ®. All rights reserved worldwide.

Cover design and page layout: Keely Wiese

Photography: Roy Wiese

First printing, 2021

Printed by DiggyPOD, Inc., in the United States of America

Published by Cynthia E. Wiese, Pennsylvania, USA

Dedicated to the Lord, my Trail Blazer,

and to Roy, my Travel Buddy.

Table of Contents

Acknowledgments		i
Author's Note		iii
Chapter 1	... swept off to ...	1
Chapter 2	... teach us lessons ...	9
Chapter 3	... don't want any adventures ...	19
Chapter 4	... the world is out there ...	27
Chapter 5	... going on an adventure ...	33
Chapter 6	... those who wander ...	43
Chapter 7	... eager feet ...	51
Chapter 8	... silly prayers ...	59
Chapter 9	... interruptions ...	69
Chapter 10	... little by little ...	75

Chapter 11	... a simple hello ...	79
Chapter 12	... friends who frequent it...	83
Chapter 13	... pleasant inns are not home ...	103
Chapter 14	... truth prevails ...	111
Chapter 15	... chosen for one another ...	119
Chapter 16	... pleasure remembered ...	127
Chapter Heading Citations		135
Additional Resources for Explorers		137

Acknowledgments

I have a greater appreciation for the gratitude that fills an author's heart for all those who helped get their book from an idea to a published copy. It truly does take a village and I want to thank my team.

So often writers who are married express profuse gratitude for their spouses. I think I know why. At least in my case, I slipped into a parallel universe as I wrote which meant that my husband, Roy, found himself picking up pieces to keep the basics in life going. He was also editor-in-chief, offering valuable input as I often sought his word-smithing advice.

My family support also included all three of my children, Craig, Scott, and Shannon, who made helpful suggestions. And Keely, my eldest granddaughter, designed the book cover, helped with page layout, and gave me a useful writing tip that shaped the entire text.

At one point I had gone over the story so many times that I couldn't see the forest for the trees and I had run out the string with Roy, who was getting as muddled as I was from becoming too familiar with the text. So as I continued through the refining process I reached out to Tine and Craig Tavani, Whitney Kuniholm, Joy Johnston, and Leslie Potter and want to thank each one of them for their gift of time and helpful suggestions. If this book does not reflect all of the good input, the fault is mine.

I would also like to thank DiggyPOD, the printing service that provided invaluable publishing and layout advice for a first-time self-publisher like me. In addition to their informative website and sample book, they were available by phone to answer my questions. I must have called them at least a dozen times and they were always friendly and helpful.

The primary credit, however, goes to the Lord, who is the author of the events that make up this story and who had been patiently prompting me to put it down in writing. I thank him for working through me to get it done and for giving me his joy in the journey.

Author's Note

An author needs to know their audience. That was a struggle for me because on the one hand I was writing primarily to the people of Písek, but on the other hand I was also writing to my English-speaking family and friends around the world. All language, including English, is tied up in culture, so I decided to start by writing to Americans as that would make it easier for me to get my thoughts down. Also, that perspective would give my Czech readers the opportunity to "listen-in" as I tell my story to Americans about my experience of moving to and living in their country. I pictured three of us conversing together — myself, an American, and a Czech whom I turn to and address directly at the end.

My next challenge was how to bring together the events of the story. Life is not a straight road and I have not written my story in a straightforward, chronological, this-follows-that format. Rather it is more like a tapestry into which I have attempted to weave the various threads that make up the whole picture of my journey to Písek. As I recounted the path's twists and turns, I sometimes had to pause and look to my more distant past before continuing. In so doing, I opted for a blend of topical and chronological approaches to connect the dots of my story.

I couldn't write about my journey without including how God led me along the way. Sometimes I refer to him as "God" and sometimes "the Lord". The names are interchangeable.

For any punctuation gurus, you may notice that I didn't follow the American rule for placement of periods and commas relative to quotation marks. Instead I followed the British rule because it makes more sense to me.

Finally, for those who don't know the background of the name "Czech Republic", a brief update may be helpful since my journey took me there.

> 1918 - Following the collapse of the Austro-Hungarian Empire at the end of WWI, Czechs and Slovaks joined together to found the independent country of Czechoslovakia.
>
> 1993 - The so-called "Velvet Divorce" resulted in the peaceful breakup of Czechoslovakia into two separate nations, the Czech Republic and the Slovak Republic, also known as Slovakia.
>
> 2013 - Two Chechen terrorists bombed the Boston Marathon. CNN incorrectly reported that the men were from the Czech Republic. The Czech ambassador had to inform CNN and the American public that Chechens were from Chechnya in Russia, not Czech Republic.

2016 - In addition to the name "Czech Republic", the country adopted "Czechia" as its official "short form" English name. But most Czech people did not embrace it and many expressed concern that the similar sound of Czechia and Chechnya would continue causing confusion.

2020 - A Euronews October 13 headline reads, "The Czech Republic is still officially called Czechia. Why hasn't it caught on?" The article states, "Indeed, survey after survey has found that most Czechs still prefer the lengthier name over the shortened one in English." Nevertheless, Czechia is now widely used internationally. If you look on Google maps, for example, you'll see Czechia instead of Czech Republic.

Since most Czechs prefer the name "Czech Republic", that's what I use. Regarding international abbreviations, within the country some Czechs use the abbreviation CR in text messages, etc. However, internationally the official country abbreviation is CZ, so I used that because CR is Costa Rica.

I hope this note has prepared the way for you to join me on my journey as I relive it through the following pages.

1

> "It's a dangerous business, Frodo,
> going out of your door," he used to say.
> "You step into the Road, and if you don't keep your feet,
> there is no knowing where you might be swept off to."
> ~ J.R.R. Tolkien

"Why are you here?"

"Because the church across the street invited us." My husband, Roy, gestured as he answered.

All the students got up and looked out the classroom window to see Církev Bratrská, the church on Tyršova. Roy was helping a Czech teacher of English by giving her students an opportunity to converse with a native English speaker.

Roy and I had been asked that same question many times and usually gave the same, superficial answer about being invited by a local church. But it was our heart's desire to have an opportunity some day to tell the whole, fascinating story, especially because many people mistakenly concluded that the reason we were there was for a sort of "retirement hobby", something to keep us from getting bored during our senior years. Yet they couldn't understand why we would move away from our family to pursue such a hobby. We agree that would not make sense.

This is the real story of why we moved to Písek in the Czech Republic (CZ). It began in Virginia one chilly November evening in 2007. We never dreamed that our lives were about to change as we walked out the door to go to the opening night of the annual Missions Conference at Reston Bible Church. You know, foreign and American Christian workers from around the world speak about what God is doing in their part of the world, share any struggles they may be dealing with, and sometimes seek volunteers for special projects. We had participated almost every year for the previous 25 years, it was something we always looked forward to, and we assumed this year would be like all the others.

That year a woman, Jackie Cross, got up to speak about her service in the Czech Republic. As she was finishing, she mentioned that a church in Prague needed volunteer native English speakers to help at an English Camp the following summer. Jackie said anyone who was interested should talk to her after the meeting.

What happened next is difficult to explain. Roy and I both immediately felt something happen inside, some inner excitement and/or understanding that this was for us. We looked at each other with eyes wide open and Roy whispered, "We're going!" I nodded. We don't usually agree instantly about many things, especially about something as significant as an international trip which we hadn't previously even thought about. But this wasn't a discussion to have or a decision to be made. It was a fact - a calling from God and we both knew it.

After the meeting we found Jackie and told her of our interest. She handed us a form on a clipboard, told us to write down our contact information, and promptly walked away. That surprised and confused us, but we were both convinced and eager so we did as she asked and began what turned out to be a long wait.

After a few weeks passed and there was no word from Jackie, we began emailing to ask for more information about the camp. For example, it would be nice to know the dates so we could buy airline tickets and schedule vacation time at work. Little things like that. Christmas, New Years, and Valentine's Day came and went. Finally we got replies, but Jackie just kept telling us to pray about whether or not we should go. We did so and continued to be convinced, but we were also increasingly concerned about the lack of the information we needed so we could make plans. We knew that Jackie was staying in the area on furlough for a few more months before returning to her Czech home in Ostrava, so we invited her to dinner so we could talk.

To our delight, we clicked. Maybe we should have tried a face-to-face meeting sooner. Jackie revealed that, in the past, she had difficult experiences with some of her fellow Americans whom she had invited to help with English

Camps, so she decided she would never do it again. But that night in November Jackie felt that God was telling her to invite volunteers. Reluctantly she obeyed him and then, just as she feared, someone responded. No wonder she walked away from Roy and me at the Mission's Conference as we stood there grinning with enthusiasm. We understood Jackie's caution and wisdom in making sure that she heard correctly from the Lord.

In July 2008 we arrived in Prague a few days before the first day of camp to recover from jet lag and help with final preparations. Jackie had meetings in Poland and couldn't join us until the first evening of camp. In her absence, the Czech camp leaders took responsibility for hosting us, which gave us the advantage of establishing a bond with them from the beginning that remains to this day and has grown stronger over the years. They were a team of about eight recent university graduates and graduate students, a bit younger than our own children. Roy and I have lived in a few different countries and our lives have been enriched by getting to know many people and experiencing a variety of cultures, such as the gentle Maasai of Kenya, the strong Afrikaaners of Dutch heritage in South Africa, and the poetic, articulate British, among others. But almost from the first day, being with Czech people caused a very different and unexpected reaction in Roy and me; we felt "at home".

When we weren't helping with camp preparations we were turned loose to explore the city and we fell in love with Prague. Unlike many other European cities, Prague was not heavily bombed in WWII so almost all of its Gothic, Renaissance, and Baroque architecture remains a feast for the eyes. This City of a Hundred Spires, as it is called, lured us into its labyrinth of very narrow streets that few cars ventured onto, which added to the pleasure of wandering about.

After a few days it was time to board the bus to the camp at a hostel in the tiny village of Paseky nad Jizerou in the Krkonoše mountains near the Polish border. Even though it wasn't the Alps, the *Sound of Music* came to mind as I looked out over the green, rolling landscape and it would not have surprised me to see the Von Trapp children march by singing *Do-Re-Mi*.

Camp was a bustle of rewarding, exhilarating, and exhausting activity, especially for people in their 50's like us as we tried to keep up with students in their late teens to early twenties. I got lost in the forest the first day. I don't have very strong lungs and we were playing a game that required a lot of running so I fell behind and lost sight of everyone. I came to a crossroads and listened. Nothing but silence. Huh. My hearing is excellent and I couldn't have been that far behind. I was confused and concerned because I didn't have a cell phone and no one seemed to know I was missing. I prayed and asked the Lord which way I should go. He directed my attention to a ribbon high overhead on a tree branch. I went that way and found the group quite close, but down in a gully that had prevented me from hearing them. Whew!

We were incredibly active every day. Generally our schedule ran along these typical lines:

- :: early morning prayer with the leaders
- :: delicious, fresh breakfast buffet
- :: English conversation and teaching in small groups
- :: lunch, the main meal of the day
- :: outdoor games, led by a very fit, extreme-sports kind of guy
- :: dinner
- :: evening program during which an English-speaking or Czech leader shared a personal faith story
- :: small group discussions which could go on late into the night

The leadership team blended their creative talent with humor and love. It was such a fun, blessed week. I didn't think it was possible for me to do so much on so little sleep, including an all-nighter the last night of camp. It had to be God's grace. On the one hand I loved every minute, but on the other I was relieved just to have survived.

Only a couple days were left for follow-up in Prague, which promised to be easier, and then I could sleep on the airplane. Sleep, beautiful sleep.... Those were the thoughts rolling through my mind the morning of the last day of camp. Before we all boarded the bus to return to Prague, Roy and I were standing in front of the group with other volunteers to receive thank you gifts. Roy took the opportunity to thank everyone and to announce, "We'll be back next year."

What! What was he thinking? We hadn't talked about it. I hadn't even thought about it. This was NOT like that night in November. I felt no calling from the Lord. There was no instant agreement. Yes, I loved camp, but at that moment I sure didn't want do it again. Groan…..

2

"God allows us to experience the low points of life in order to teach us lessons that we could learn in no other way."

~ C.S. Lewis

After camp we returned to our home in northern Virginia and many things were happening simultaneously. I was busy at work, busy trying to finish renovations on our house, and busy preparing to take in four children, ages 8-16. One of my sisters, Ellen, was a struggling single mom who lived in Wisconsin, about 850 miles away. Shortly after their divorce, her ex-husband left and moved to Florida. Ellen needed extended time to focus on her own personal recovery, so the children were staying temporarily with a foster family but needed a longer term solution. Roy and I were a logical family option, but we could only care for the children if we became legal guardians and they moved to our house.

We had begun to head down that path before English Camp, including getting approved by social services in Virginia. Now that we were back from camp we had a lot to do to get ready. Seventeen years earlier Roy and I bought our house, a handyman special. I knew it needed a ton of work, but I naively thought that in a year or two we'd have it fully repaired and redecorated. There I was, seventeen years later, rushing to finally finish before our nieces and nephews moved in. Never mind that our own children had grown up in a home with a kitchen wall exposing studs, pipes, and electric wires.

After launching our own children I was wondering how I was going to cope with what felt like a very unnatural return to parenthood. Since I was already feeling my age, I wasn't sure I was up to caring for Ellen's children for an undetermined amount of time.

As we continued making preparations I found myself reminiscing about raising our own kids. Like most young mothers I had often been encouraged by older, more experienced mothers to cherish the child-rearing years because they pass so quickly. I always nodded in acknowledgement but never really took it to heart. I suppose it was because I was often exhausted when our children were young. Our first born, Craig, was 3 1/2 and Scott was 19 months old when our daughter, Shannon, was born. Now, as I look back on those precious years when they lived at home, I agree wholeheartedly with the wise women who counseled me and I cherish the memories of those days.

As a child, Craig was shy and quiet. When he was about six years old I called a neighbor and asked to borrow an egg. She lived in the same townhouse building about four doors down the sidewalk. I asked Craig to go get it for me while I continued cooking, assuring him he wouldn't have to talk much because the neighbor already knew he was coming for the egg. Craig disappeared and a minute later I heard him in the other room quietly instructing four-year old Scott, "I'll knock on the door, you ask for the egg, and I'll carry it home." Who knew he would grow up to become an astute business developer and consultant with a gift for communication?

Scott was an inquisitive child whose preferred method of satisfying his curiosity was the hands-on, plunge-in, think-later method. Unknown to me, when we were living in South Africa for two years while Roy was serving at the US Embassy in Pretoria, one burning question in Scott's five-year-old mind was, "What would it feel like to have hamsters in my shirt?" Obviously, the only way to find out was to tuck his shirt into his shorts and drop his two pet hamsters down the neck. The hamsters tickled him as they ran laps around his waist, much to Scott's amusement. He found the experiment so successful that he repeated it again and again over the following few days. I had no idea about his new source of entertainment or that it was the cause of a strange rash ring around his waist. I had been worrying that the rash was some exotic African parasite. Then one day I heard Scott giggling and went to see what was so funny. Medical mystery solved and pets rescued. Scott's hands-on approach led him to a career in medicine in which he now thinks first before plunging in.

Shannon is our tender-hearted animal lover. When she was five, I found her outside one day after a heavy rain.

She had set up a worm hospital for all the worms that washed up out of the soil. Shannon is also the family artist who got out her crayons, scissors, and glue to turn her first grade math test into a 3-D sculpture for the teacher. So it wasn't surprising she was selected to study interior design at a highly competitive university program. Although she is not currently working in that field, she has a gift for making beautiful things out of the ordinary.

As new Christians, Roy and I had raised our children in a Christian home and expected all of us to live happily ever after. But as teenagers, each child asserted their independence by distancing themself from the Lord in their own, unique way. They needed to know what they believed for themselves and not because of our influence, which was wise. By God's grace, over time each of them chose to follow Jesus. There is no greater joy for a Christian parent.

At the same time we were experiencing stress for many years caused by repeated attacks of acute pancreatitis that both Scott and Shannon suffered. Flare-ups of pancreatic inflammation are extremely painful and require having nothing to eat or drink, not even water, for about a week so the pancreas can rest and the inflammation can subside. This requires being hospitalized and put on IV fluids to prevent dehydration.

Our worst crisis was in January 2001. We were living in England while Roy was on assignment there. Back in the States Scott was a senior at the College of William & Mary and over Christmas break he had an exploratory procedure called an ERCP under anesthesia. I wanted to fly home to be with Scott during the procedure, but he insisted he didn't need me there and the pancreatic specialist agreed that it was a relatively simple procedure and Scott should be fine. However, during the procedure the IV slipped out of Scott's vein, he woke up from the anesthesia, sat up on the operating table, and pulled the endoscope out of his mouth. Rather than going back to his dormitory room, as originally expected, Scott was admitted to a step-down intensive care unit with acute pancreatitis. It is possible that the interrupted ERCP was only coincidental to his pancreatic flare-up and not the cause. It didn't matter. Once I heard that Scott was hospitalized, I got on the next plane to be with him. After about a week he seemed to be improving and was sent back to school. But within a few days he was in pain and was admitted to a smaller, local hospital near his college in Williamsburg, Virginia.

The gastroenterologist (GI doctor) ordered a CT scan which shows more detail than a regular x-ray, including organs and tissues. Given the results, the doctor told Scott he wasn't going to be able to finish his school year and would have to apply for a medical withdrawal. Since it was Scott's senior year, that also meant he wasn't going to be able to graduate with his friends and would have to finish his final semester the next school year. The disappointing news caused Scott's eyes to fill with tears. A pastor from his church happened to be visiting at that time and tried to console Scott by telling him not to worry and adding something like, "Who knows. Maybe God is going to have you meet the girl you're going to marry." But Scott wasn't encouraged and he asked his pastor to have the elders come and pray for his healing, as it says in the Bible, "Is anyone among you sick? Let him call for the elders of the church, and let them pray over him, anointing him with oil in the name of the Lord." (James 5:14)

A week later Scott was in desperate condition. The GI doctor ordered another CT scan which revealed a large phlegmon (inflammation of his soft tissues and a lot of pus) that filled his peritoneal cavity and a large cyst that squeezed Scott's stomach in half. The doctor decided to try a course of antibiotics.

Roy had remained in Europe and communication in those days was difficult, so I was alone and in agony as I began to fear that Scott might not survive. I fervently prayed that the Lord would rescue him, but I eventually came to a point with the Lord where I submitted to his will and "let go" of Scott. Because of the gift of eternal life through Jesus, I knew that if Scott died, he would literally be in a better place where I would eventually join him. Peaceful agony is the only way I can describe how I felt at that time.

Although Scott needed to be on medication, he didn't need to be in the hospital so the doctor discharged him with a special, large IV called a PICC-line through which four smaller IV lines ran. I had to manage all of them around the clock: IV fluids, nutrition, antibiotics, and morphine.

The morphine was on-demand so that when Scott had pain he could push a button and get some relief. Of course it was regulated so he couldn't get too much at once.

A week after his discharge Scott had an appointment with the pancreatic specialist who did the ERCP at the larger regional hospital in Richmond. I brought the week-old CT scans and the specialist gasped when he saw the films. After taking a deep breath, he questioned all his medical students who were in the room. And then, to my surprise, he asked my opinion. Also to my surprise, the words that came out of my mouth were, "He is better."

Wait! Did I just say that?! I hadn't even been aware that Scott WAS getting better. When did it happen? The specialist pointed to each of his students and said, "Mom says he's better."

Then he swung into action and ordered emergency surgery to cut away the dead tissue in hopes they would find enough healthy tissue remaining to regenerate. He put his residents to work arranging the surgery. He also ordered another set of films so the surgeon would have up-to-date knowledge of what he would find when he operated.

Our first instruction was to go up to the 9th floor where Scott would be admitted as an in-patient. The elevators were notoriously slow and Scott needed the toilet, so we ran up the stairs. Laughing and stumbling, I was trying to keep up with him because I was carrying his IV bags.

Yikes! "Wait for me, Scott!" Was this is the same guy who was in such desperate condition last week?? Later I realized Scott wasn't having pain so he wasn't pushing his morphine button and instead had begun going through withdrawal. That, combined with having been on antibiotics, was why he had to make a mad dash to the bathroom and found the energy to sprint up nine flights of stairs.

Shortly after Scott got settled in his room he was taken to radiology and I went down to the cafeteria for a break. As I was returning to his room I decided that one trip up the stairs was enough that day, and while I was waiting for one of the slow elevators, one of the medical students came running up to me asking if I had heard the news. No, I hadn't. "We're not going to do the surgery. Scott is completely healed! It's a miracle!"

Impossible! Completely healed? But those CT films from last week... Wow! I was speechless. Even though the elders from Scott's church never had a chance to come and pray over him, I believe that God honored Scott's faith and healed him. I have read about such things in the Bible but never dreamed something like it could happen to us. Breathtaking thankfulness! And what a buzz the story created in the hospital!

Scott's healing was amazing, to be sure, but he was left with his original pancreatic problem and continued to have periodic flare-ups. Even those episodes improved after an additional health problem was solved. When Scott was young he picked up a parasite in South Africa. Tropical disease medicine is not widely practiced in the US. It was many years and hospitalizations later before the parasite was accurately identified and treated. Shannon was found to have the same parasite and was treated as well. After treatment both of them seemed to improve and have fewer acute pancreatic attacks. Was there a connection or was it just a coincidence? We don't know. Their condition was still a concern, but we were so grateful to God for the progress.

Oh, and as it turned out, by having to return to school in the autumn to finish his college degree in Information Technology, Scott did meet his future wife, Jan, who was an incoming freshman. He says that going through the crisis proved to be one of the best things that ever happened to him because of all the good that came out of it, including his subsequent decision to go back to school to study medicine and become a doctor.

So in 2008 Roy and I were simultaneously recovering from those family health crises while enjoying the next phase of life as all three of our children had married, settled in their own homes, and begun making us grandparents. But at the same time, we were making preparations to take care of Ellen's children and begin a return to parenthood. That was our situation as we returned from our first English Camp.

3

> "Sorry! I don't want any adventures, thank you. Not Today.
> Good morning!
> But please come to tea — any time you like!
> Why not tomorrow? Come tomorrow!
> Good-bye!"
> ~ J.R.R. Tolkien

After returning from camp Roy kept talking about spending summers in Prague to do more English Camps and work with university students, to which I always silently responded, "Whatever." I was too distracted by the prospect of becoming guardians for Ellen's children to seriously consider Roy's pipe dream.

I need to pause and describe the background for what happened next. For the past 40 years Roy and I have begun the day by independently spending time reading the Bible and praying. That communication with God is essential to us. When we were new Christians we did it because a more mature Christian told us we should and we agreed that it would be a nice thing to do, but as the years have gone by and the Lord has taken us down many different roads, we have come to the conclusion that it is necessary for our very survival, as well as being an immense treasure. It is food for the soul, light and wisdom for the path, strength for the journey, courage for the battle, correction for when we need it, balm for our wounds, hope for our future. It is Jesus himself in written form, "The Word became flesh and made his dwelling among us." (John 1:14)

Our approach is to simply start reading at the beginning of the Bible in Genesis, prayerfully read a bit, mark the page with a bookmark, and that's where we begin the next morning. I don't know how many times we've each read through the entire Bible that way over the years. Most often the Lord communicates general revelation that is for all people. But sometimes he seems to "breathe life" into specific words so that they almost "jump off the page" or resonate "audibly" in our minds as God communicates something personal and specific apart from its general context.

On the morning of November 18, 2008 Roy told me the Lord "spoke" in that special way to him, " ... I looked, and there before me was a door standing open... ." (Revelation 4:1) Then Roy left for work.

What!?

What door?

I needed to know more!

And as soon as possible!

I had been talking to Roy about inviting Ellen to move in with us along with her children while she recovered. He didn't think it was a good idea. So I thought maybe that was the door that God was opening. You know, that he was helping Roy change his mind. I tried to email my sister, not to invite her, but just to see if communicating with her gave me any clues.

My computer kept freezing. I tried again and again. Same thing. Once more. Still wouldn't work. "OK I give up!" Arghhh! I shut the whole thing down.

While it was rebooting, I felt ridiculous. I got on my knees and told the Lord I was sorry and that I would relax, quit pounding on closed doors, and that he could show me the open door whenever he wanted to.

I was calmer as I logged back onto my computer and into email where a new message loaded. It was from Ondra, one of the English Camp leaders from Prague.

```
"Dear Roy & Cindy,
……… When you go to wikipedia and search for
religions, the Czech is a small black gap
inside Europe. I do not know why is it so..
We hope to see you again sometimes in
Czech !!"
```

I was stunned! I was humbled and thankful for the Lord's kindness to satisfy my curiosity so quickly. The "door" wasn't about Ellen, but he did make it very clear that we should do English Camp again. And maybe even spend summers in Prague. Maybe.

Meanwhile, as time was drawing near for our nieces and nephews to move in with us, we learned that they preferred to stay with the foster family. That's putting it mildly. We found out that Laura, 15 years old, secured the services of a *guardian ad litem* to fight against having to move to Virginia because she wanted to stay in Wisconsin near her friends and her mom. And the foster parents wanted the children to stay with them and had filed the documents to become guardians for the children, which would compete with our petition to become their guardians.

We were confused. We loved those kids and we were family. In addition to normal family love and loyalty, this Bible verse had been a general source of guidance from the beginning, "Anyone who does not provide for their relatives, and especially for their own household, has denied the faith and is worse than an unbeliever." (1 Timothy 5:8)

Despite the new obstacles, and as Roy and I were praying about what to do, we continued making preparations for their arrival. We needed a van with enough seats for all of us to travel together, so Roy found a used one that looked promising. On the same day that we were going to go look at the van, as I was tidying up the house and putting things away, I "happened" to pick up an extra Bible on the coffee table and I "happened" to open to this verse, "Leave your orphans behind; I will do what is needed..." (Jeremiah 49:11 AMP) The Lord struck my heart with that unique verse. Most often in Scripture we are instructed to take care of orphans. Our nieces and nephews felt like orphans to us, **our** orphans, because they needed healthy parental care. Yet the Lord clearly guided us to let go and he would take good care of them. What timing!

How we appreciated the gift of that precise, personal direction at the time we so desperately needed it. I thought back to Ecclesiastes 3:1, "There is a time for everything, and a season for every activity under the heavens..."

God knew what time it was, what the situation called for. We didn't buy the van. And instead of having the children move in with us, we supported them staying with the foster family. That was at the end of 2008 and the Lord has done what he said he would do. All four kids have grown up and are doing well. They are loving, hard-working adults and we are proud of each one.

Life seemed to be settling down to normal, not my usual kind of "normal" but the kind of normal I imagined other people had. Scott and Shannon seemed fairly healthy, we finished the work on the house, and my nieces and nephews were being well cared for. We had a normal Christmas and normal New Years welcoming 2009.

On the morning of January 11 I was still basking in my new normal. With a hot cup of tea in hand I curled up in my cozy corner with my Bible and my journal as I did every morning. After reading and praying, I would jot down Scripture, thoughts, and prayers in a sort of letter-to-God format based on what I had just read and what was going on in my life. That morning I had just read about the people who were building the Tower of Babel in Genesis 11:4. "Then they said, 'Come, let us build ourselves a city, with a tower that reaches to the heavens, so that we may ... not be scattered over the face of the whole earth.'" I could identify with them wanting to stay right where they were as I wrote in my journal,

I confess that the same can be said of me more often than I like. Please help me be driven to glorify your name and go where you want. Even with my interest in CZ, I still love my home. Especially the more we fix it up and the more beautiful and comfortable it is, the more tempted I am to want to indulge in being here. Please help me glorify your name & go where you want. Thank you.

I have to tell you that until just now as I copied those words from my journal onto this page, I had no memory whatsoever of praying (twice!) that the Lord would help me go where he wanted. Really? I must have meant it but I sure don't remember praying it very seriously. I remember being more focused on enjoying my new normal than on being scattered somewhere.

Anyway, given my frame of mind, maybe you can imagine my shock the very next morning when the following words jumped off the page. "Leave your country and your people ... and go to the country that I will show you ... I will bless you." (Genesis 12:1-2 ERV)

GASP! How many times had I read those very words over the years? But never before had they hit me like a bolt of lightening as they did that morning. I wrote in my journal,

January 12, 2009
Dear Father, Is it possible that this is what you are saying to me? I was fully prepared to do summer camp, but this kind of commitment catches me by surprise. I will do what you ask, but please make it very clear by showing Roy independently. ...

I was in shock and turmoil as I tried to gently push away the idea of moving to the Czech Republic.

4

*"Tell me. When did doilies and your mother's dishes become so important to you? I remember a young hobbit who was always running off in search of Elves in the woods. He'd stay out late, come home after dark, trailing mud and twigs and fireflies. A young hobbit who would've liked nothing better than to find out what was beyond the borders of the Shire.
The world is not in your books and maps. It's out there."*
~ Gandalf

I kept the inner turmoil to myself over the next couple of months. I didn't speak a word of it to anyone, especially not to Roy. Instead, I continuously, nervously asked the Lord to give me clarification and/or confirmation to show me if I understood him correctly or not.

I had questions and concerns. What about Scott's and Shannon's health? Sure they were better, but they weren't completely healed and whenever either of them was hospitalized, I usually needed to help on the home front or be at their bedside. And what about learning such a difficult language when I was too old for that? What about my respiratory weakness? What about finances? For many years of our marriage we scraped along living paycheck-to-paycheck but finally had well-paying jobs. Were we supposed to walk away from that, especially during the peak of a global financial crisis and Great Recession that had begun in 2007? These questions and more tumbled around my mind.

What a patient and kind heavenly Father we have, who knows our hearts and thoughts better than we ourselves and is willing and able to give us what we need in due season! I wasn't sure how to explain how he answered my prayers for confirmation, so I decided to just share some notes from my journal entries.

January 17, 2009
"So Sarah laughed to herself as she thought, 'After I am worn out … will what the Lord says really happen?' Then the LORD said, ' … Is anything too hard for the LORD?'" (Genesis 18:12-14) Sarah's disbelief was based on her own weakness, but she forgot to finish her analysis and consider the power of the Lord to do what he says he will do. I am guilty of Sarah's same mistake. Please help me believe you and walk accordingly. Thank you.

I remember really identifying with the worn out feeling and even found it underlined in my journal. Ha ha! That brought the "too old to learn" concern to the forefront of my mind and the Lord struck my heart with those words, giving me the correction and encouragement I needed.

January 24, 2009

"'... he will send his angel before you ...' Then the man bowed down and worshiped the LORD, saying, 'Praise be to the LORD'" (...) "'The LORD, before whom I have walked faithfully, will send his angel with you and make your journey a success ...'" (Genesis 24:7, 26, & 40) Is the journey to CZ? That is the obvious one that comes to mind.

January 28, 2009

"I am with you and will watch over you wherever you go..." (Genesis 28:15)

"... 'God will be with me and will watch over me on this journey...'" (Genesis 28:20)

February 5, 2009

"Then the LORD said to Jacob, 'Go back to the land of your fathers and to your relatives, and I will be with you.'" (Genesis 31:3)

I didn't know what to make of this verse at the time, but it struck me so I recorded it in my journal anyway. Ten years later I discovered that I apparently do have ancestors from south Bohemia, my great-grandmother (my mother's father's mother) whose family name was Novák.

While I was wrestling with the whole idea of moving to CZ, in the back of my mind I had been thinking that living in a city would be tough because of my weak lungs. So if we were really called to move, it would probably be better to live in a smaller town where the air might be cleaner. That was if we were going to live in CZ at all.

We received a letter from Jackie, who had returned to her home in Ostrava in eastern CZ after her furlough in the US, and I read it late that night. She wrote that some churches in smaller towns and villages were asking for missionaries to join them in their service and she requested prayer that the Lord would send people. That specific request took my breath away. I quickly put the letter aside and tried to put the thought of moving out of my mind. However, God had other plans as you can see from my journal entry the following morning.

February 6, 2009, Friday
Wow. Your call is quite clear. ... I read Jackie's letter last night and you struck my heart with the specific request for help in one of the towns in CZ. I was trying to clear my mind and stop thinking about the Czech Republic so I could sleep. I picked up a new book to read on a completely different subject so I could try to distract myself. But what was right there, the first thing on the first page? "Leave your country and your people ... and go to the land I will show you... I will bless you." (Genesis 12:1-2 ERV) This morning, before fully waking up, I was restless with a question relentlessly rolling around my mind. It was similar to a question in Paul's letter to the Romans, "... and how can they go unless they are sent?" "... and how can they go unless they are sent?" "... and how can they go unless they are

sent?" So this morning I opened my Bible and this "happened" to be the first thing I read, "'Come, I am going to send you to them.' 'Very well,' he replied.'" (Genesis 37:13) Only by your grace can I say, "Very well." But, by Your grace, I will. Thank you.

I remember feeling a sense of relief. The inner struggle was over and I was free. Once again I felt the Lord's peace and joy - and even a little excitement about moving to CZ.

I knew I had to break my silence with Roy. On Sunday afternoon, not knowing how he would react I began cautiously revealing how the Lord was leading me, and when I finally got to the main point, Roy smiled, picked up a Bible, opened to one of the front pages, and pointed to a faint watermark phrase, "Therefore go..." (Matthew 28:19 TNIV)

Little did I know that while I was keeping my thoughts to myself, the Lord had been having his own conversations with Roy. Then I remembered. Back in January when I was in shock the morning I read, "Leave your country...." and while I was reeling from the very thought of moving, I prayed and asked God that if he really was telling us to move and it wasn't my imagination, would he please tell Roy independently without me mentioning a thing about it. It turned out that God answered the prayer that I had forgotten I prayed.

In fact, Roy had long wanted to go part-time, but then had been feeling that the Lord was asking him to go full-time.

That was another matter because Roy had been concerned about the financial implications of completely quitting his job. He had been planning to work for several more years to save for retirement, but then it occurred to him that he already had a pension and God graciously showed him that we had enough. It was that same Sunday morning, before I broke my silence with Roy in the afternoon, that the Lord struck his heart with the words, "Therefore go..." And so it was settled, and what a relief it was to be in-step and able to talk with each other about what was foremost on our minds!

It's interesting that at the beginning of this chapter I wrote that I was in turmoil for a couple of months, but clearly it was less than one month. I guess my lack of peace made time seem to drag.

Although we had shared our recognition of God's call with each other, we kept it to ourselves for a while. I suppose that, subconsciously, the act of telling other people, especially our children, took it to a new level of commitment and I guess we were a little hesitant.

5

"I'm going on an adventure!"
~ Bilbo Baggins

Even though the call seemed so clear, I was really struggling with leaving our children and grandchildren because I loved them so much and wanted to be with them and I thought they needed us. Even the idea of telling them was daunting. Yet again, I really needed the Lord to reassure me, and he did. Here is a sample from my journal of my conversations with him about my concerns. In the first entry I note a strange connection I felt with Jacob.

February 22, 2009
"'... I am about to die, but God will be with you...'" (Genesis 48:21) Jacob was facing a more long-term separation and he was comforted and gave comfort on the basis of your presence with his children. Knowing you will be with our children and grandchildren brings great comfort. Thank you!

February 25
You are addressing my other concern ... my ability to learn the language at my age. Moses was worried about his inability to speak eloquently, "'... I have never been eloquent ...' The LORD said to

him, 'Who gave human beings their mouths? Who makes them deaf or mute? Who gives them sight or makes them blind? Is it not I, the LORD? Now go; I will help you speak and will teach you what to say.'" (Exodus 4:10-11)

March 18
... that nagging fear about Scott and Shannon's health rose up in me. This morning you showed me this, "'... I will take away sickness from among you ...'" (Exodus 23:25) May it be so! Thank you!

There was much more but you get the idea. Roy and I began taking small steps of faith. By mid-March we had told all of our children and grandchildren. That was difficult because we knew it wasn't going to be easy for any of us. They were surprised, but very supportive. We also told Jackie and a few friends at church. Even so, I had some lingering doubts and was almost subconsciously holding on to the thought that I could still back out.

A welcome sign of spring in Washington DC is the Cherry Blossom Festival. In 1912 the Japanese gave our country 3,000 cherry trees as a token of friendship. Even though we had lived in the area for over 25 years we never went to the festival, but the prospect of moving inspired us not to waste another opportunity. Besides, it was a chance to clear our minds. We enjoyed the beautiful April morning strolling under a canopy of pink blossoms alongside the Tidal Basin.

Leaving the cherry blossoms and water's edge, we continued our walk through the adjacent Franklin Roosevelt Memorial in its park-like setting.

We followed the path around a corner and

stopped dead in our tracks.

> THE ONLY LIMIT TO OUR REALIZATION OF TOMORROW WILL BE OUR DOUBTS OF TODAY LET US MOVE FORWARD WITH STRONG AND ACTIVE FAITH

THE ONLY LIMIT TO OUR REALIZATION OF TOMORROW
WILL BE OUR DOUBTS OF TODAY
LET US MOVE FORWARD WITH STRONG AND ACTIVE FAITH

Those words, literally etched in stone, knocked the last vestige of doubt out of me.

We officially informed our church, which made it feel like a real commitment on our part. Churches are like families and just as families have different personalities, so our church, Reston Bible Church, had its special identity — a focus on sharing the good news in the Bible with people around the world; that is, with anyone who was interested. It all started in the late 1970's when one inspired man suggested that our church support a couple of missionaries. That decision grew over the years into an international program that supported over 250 missionaries in over 50 countries, many of whom were foreign nationals serving their fellow citizens. To provide proper care and oversight of that ministry, the church had a committee that worked on the home front to ensure that workers sent abroad were genuine Christians and not "wolves in sheep's clothing", that they were communicating God's message faithfully, and that they were given adequate support. That job was made more efficient through the use of mission agencies that acted as intermediaries between the missionary on the field and the home church.

Interestingly, one of the first questions most people at church asked Roy and me when they heard our news was what mission agency we would join. We had no idea it was such a big deal, but we figured we would just go with the same one Jackie belonged to. And so our move to the Czech Republic was underway.

6

"Not all those who wander are lost..."
~ J.R.R. Tolkien

July 2009 arrived before we knew it and we found ourselves back at Paseky for camp. Most of the same leaders from our first camp were there. We were all preparing for the arrival of the students the following day, and as we were seated in a circle to discuss final preparations, Roy and I announced to the group that the Lord had shown us to move to the Czech Republic. The enthusiasm and encouragement of the leaders was heartwarming.

Throughout the week, as time permitted, we met with each of the leaders as individuals or couples and asked them to tell us whatever they thought we needed to know. There was clearly a common theme — don't come with a mission agency, just come and be one of us. It made a lot of sense so we agreed. One Czech leader mentioned that one of his friends was moving to Chicago for the same reason that we were moving to CZ, to tell people the good things God had done for her. It occurred to us that it was as if God was inviting us to participate in a Christian foreign exchange program.

After camp we planned to explore smaller towns in Moravia, the eastern part of the country, where Jackie lived and we thought we might live as well. The night before our trip we had arranged to have dinner with Miriam, one of Roy's student helpers from the previous year. She couldn't be at camp that year because she was busy preparing for her wedding the following week. She wanted to see us and introduce her fiancé, Jírka. They were so cute together. You know what I mean ... young lovers a week away from their wedding day. We were very happy for both of them. When we shared our news, they, like some of the other leaders and students, invited us to live in their town, Písek, but we declined their kind offer because Písek was not in the east.

It was with eager anticipation the following morning that we set out on our exploration. We had been praying for "trail markers," as we called them, those blazes on trees, rocks, fence posts, etc. that guide hikers along the right path. We didn't mean literal trail markers. It was a word picture for our request that the Lord would give us clear guidance about where to settle. We rented a car and drove to Ostrava to pick up Jackie and begin our search. We visited villages like Šumperk and towns like Olomouc. Some people really wanted us to join them; one wasn't sure. The bottom line was that nothing, and I mean **nothing**, seemed like the right place. Not that the people weren't kind, they were extremely kind and gracious. Not that the places weren't appealing, they were. It's just that nothing felt like a match for us. It's hard to explain. We just knew we didn't fit in any of those places. I was very disappointed because I really thought the Lord was going to show us where we were going to live, but it was too late because we had to drop Jackie off and go back to Prague to catch our flight home the next morning. Sigh.

Before going to the airport hotel where we were staying that night, we had to stop in Prague at the church in Vinohrady where we had left extra luggage. We also wanted to meet with a couple we hadn't yet talked to for their opinion and advice, Ondra and Eva, the same Ondra from Prague who sent that email back in November inviting us to come again.

Ondra asked us about our trip and if the Lord showed us where we were going to live. Roy was quite cheerful as he replied that the Lord hadn't but that he had learned a lot. Roy is often content to just gather information and he was confident the Lord would show us at the right time. I was less cheerful as I expressed my disappointment. I was even starting to feel a bit claustrophobic about the whole idea of moving to Czech.

Then Ondra said something like, "You know, there isn't as much need for Christian workers where you went. There is much more of a need south and west of Prague than there is out east."

That was it! It felt like somebody opened the window and a fresh breeze blew in. I could breathe again! The sun was shining, the birds were singing! Of course I am being a bit poetic here and I know it sounds melodramatic, but the contrast was stunning even though we had never been south and west of Prague. The Lord was showing us the next trail marker and that was enough. He showed us the area, even if not the exact place, and I was so very grateful.

When we told Ondra about the advice we had been given to just come and be one of them rather than come through a mission agency, he agreed, but strongly recommended that we also get our church's blessing. Of course, we wanted that, too.

The next morning on the airplane Roy asked, "Hey, don't Miriam and Jírka live south of Prague? Isn't that where Písek is?" I didn't know.

The first morning after we had arrived back home I got out our paper map (remember those?) and found Písek, about 100 km south of Prague. I liked it! Just from its location on the map, I liked it. Prague, Munich, and Vienna formed a triangle with Písek in the middle.

I googled Písek and found that it was a town with lots of secondary schools. In fact, one website said it was a town of students and retirees. We liked that, too, especially since Roy used to teach at a university and would be a retiree when we moved.

We decided to pray about it for a couple months before mentioning it to anyone else. During that time an attachment seemed to grow in us for this town we had never seen. Eventually we wrote to Ondra to tell him that

we thought Písek might be the place. He replied that he knew a Dutch-American, Bert, who had been living there with his American wife and serving at a church called Elim for seven years, but they recently had to move back to California. We wrote to Bert introducing ourselves, telling him we were exploring the possibility of moving to Písek, and asking for any insight or advice he might have.

On October 14 we received his reply:

```
Hi Roy and Cindy,
That is an answer to prayer! We have been
trying to find a couple to replace us.
```

Needless to say, that was quite an encouragement! Bert also had lots of questions for which we had few answers because at that time we were still finding our way. But his email was a clear trail marker so we took the next step and wrote to Miriam to tell her about our change in plans and that we thought we were supposed to live in Písek, after all. We also told her that we were planning to visit in early December.

On November 2 this was her reply:

Hi Roy and Cindy,

It is nice to hear from you again. I am sorry for my late respond. We were on holiday with Jírka and came back home last week.

I am excited to hear updates from you regarding Lord´s leading you to the Czech Republic. Jírka and I are praying for you to recognize the "trail markers". We spoke to our pastor yesterday about you and he would like to meet with you when you are in the Czech Republic. He will be praying for you and for our church to know whether your place would be within our church. He said that he has been thinking recently that it could be a good thing to have Americans in the church as through English we could reach new people. This pastor (Ondřej) came to the Písek church 2 years ago and had a good experience with American missionaries from his previous church, therefore he is open to the possibility of you working with us. Ondřej is 32 years old and he and his wife both grew up in non-Christian families. It seems to us that it may be a good idea if you live in

Písek and help us to reach people here. We will be praying for recognizing God´s plan for you and for the church.

Wow! It was great encouragement to get the next trail marker through such specific confirmation. It was so cool that this pastor in Písek had been thinking the same thing the Lord seemed to be telling Roy and me to do. We were even more excited about our upcoming trip.

7

> "The Road goes ever on and on
> Down from the door where it began.
> Now far ahead the Road has gone,
> And I must follow, if I can,
> Pursuing it with eager feet,
> Until it joins some larger way
> Where many paths and errands meet.
> And whither then? I cannot say"
> ~ J.R.R. Tolkien

Even the cold, gray drizzle couldn't dampen our spirits that late December afternoon when we drove into Písek for the first time. It was already dusk as we found our way to the Villa Conti, a small, cozy hotel at the edge of the forest. After getting settled in our room, we went to Miriam and Jírka's flat for dinner and to meet Ondřej, the pastor of their church whom Miriam wrote about in her email. To be clear, this Ondřej was not the same man as Ondra, the camp leader from Prague. Ondřej was originally from Liberec in the north and had been an architecture student when he attended a Christian English Camp and met his wife, Tereza. It was through that experience that Ondřej became a follower of Jesus. Tereza couldn't join us for dinner that night so we would have to meet her another time, but Ondřej brought his toddler son, Jonáš. For dessert Miriam took vanilla wafers and put a slice of banana on each one. Then she poured melting chocolate over the top which hardened into a soft shell. They were delicious! You should try it. I was amused that Ondřej allowed Jonáš to eat so many of them. Ondřej may have read my thoughts as I couldn't contain my smile. He looked at me with a twinkle in his eye and said, "Mother isn't here." Some things are universal.

We were drawn to Ondřej's warmth. Over the course of the evening he seemed to grow more comfortable with us and confided that he had been praying that the Lord would send an American couple to the church to teach English to help with outreach. He went on to say that he hadn't even told Tereza about his prayer. The perfect match of his prayer with the Lord's guidance in our lives was a clear trail marker.

The next morning we were treated to our first breakfast at Villa Conti, a generous assortment of fresh eggs, bread, ham, cheese, yogurt, fruit, muesli, sweet rolls, juice, coffee, tea. Delicious! I was stuffed as I trudged back up the stairs to our room. Halfway up I paused on the landing to look out the window at the forest. And what did I see through the winter mist? Two trail markers on a tree! Real trail markers. I had to laugh! I thought it was amusing that the Lord gave us another trail marker, literally. It was like a sweet little joke and answer to our prayers all rolled up together.

Miriam came by to take us on a tour of the center of town. As we walked along we were delighted to discover that Písek was a beautiful, historic town straddling the Otava River. "The stone bridge is the oldest stone bridge in Central Europe," we were told.

Písek was an ancient royal town settled by Celtic peoples who panned for gold in the river. Other history of interest was closer to home. There was a monument to the U.S. Army commemorating the liberation of Písek from Nazi occupation on 6 May 1945. And, to our continued amusement, there were trail markers everywhere.

I had never seen so many trail markers in a town before.

The damp chill in the December air made the place we stopped for lunch, Hotel Biograf, all the more welcoming. Fabulous food, pleasant atmosphere, and professional, friendly service from Nouri, our server.

The next morning during breakfast at Villa Conti a light snow was beginning to fall. As we walked up the stairs to our room, I paused again to look out the window at the trail marker that beckoned from the forest. "Let's see where it leads." We followed the markers along the snow-dusted trail until we came to an opening and halted abruptly. After a few seconds I said, "I don't know what I'm looking at." It was sort of a fairy village with little houses and proportionately little dirt roads, not really meant for cars, more for walking from one little house to another and back out to the forest. "What is it?" I asked Roy. He didn't know. Whatever it was, it sure was cool. Later we learned the miniature village was a group of garden plots for people who lived in flats in town, just as we have in America, but each plot also had something between a potting shed and a cottage which gave it the appearance of a fairy village.

There was only one disappointment that visit — the air. There had been an inversion and, from the hillside outside the hotel, we looked down into town and saw that the air was tinged yellow from pollution. Because of my weak lungs, I was concerned, but the kindness of the people, the beauty of the place, the forest full of trails, the hope of better weather, and all the trail markers everywhere put that concern out of mind.

It was settled. We were moving to Písek.

8

"If God had granted all the silly prayers I've made in my life, where should I be now?"

~ C.S. Lewis

Back home, as 2009 drew to a close, we needed the Lord's step-by-step guidance to navigate logistics and timing. When should we go? Next autumn? Or wait until after Christmas? When should we resign from our jobs? What should we do about our home in Virginia? How should we prepare to teach English since neither of us was very qualified even though we had some experience? What kind of visa should we apply for? And a hundred other questions.

We decided we would quit our jobs in the spring so we could spend two months over the summer in the Czech Republic making the necessary arrangements at that end. At that point we expected to move to Písek in the autumn.

Sometime in March my company was reviewing new contract bids, so I informed them that I'd be resigning at the end of May. I thought it was only fair for them to have that information as part of their decision making. In fact, a new contract was signed in April and I wasn't included for obvious reasons. I had just enough time to tie up loose ends before leaving work and then it was a blessing to be free a month earlier to focus on our transition.

It was more difficult for Roy to give up his job. After doing graduate study at Yale, Roy's first career was teaching economics at Union College in Schenectady, New York where he had previously been an undergraduate student. Then he joined the U.S. Government and served as a diplomat and foreign affairs specialist. After retiring from government service, he worked as a private consultant/advisor to the government. Even though Roy gave his notice in January, they hadn't been able to find a replacement and begged him to stay, but he had decided his last day would be at the end of May. As I mentioned earlier, it was especially challenging to give up that job in a bad economy. He also had to face the awkward situation of telling colleagues who didn't know the Lord that God "showed" him to quit his job and move to the Czech Republic to teach English through a local church. Interestingly, it sparked an interest in some to hear more about his faith.

That took care of our jobs, but what about our house? The Lord had the perfect solution. Scott's former health crisis in 2001 had awakened in him an interest in medicine. After he graduated from college and worked only two months as an Information Technology Specialist, he decided to quit his job and go back to school to become a doctor, an anesthesiologist to be exact. When he was finishing medical school he had to apply for an internship/residency program. To his delight, he had gotten his first choice — an internship at the University of Virginia's hospital in Charlottesville, VA followed by a 3-year residency program at Georgetown Hospital in Washington, DC. The timing for his residency at Georgetown coincided with the timing of our move. The perfect solution was for him and his small family to live in our home. They didn't have to find a place they could afford in such a high-rent district as northwest DC, and we didn't have to find reliable tenants or try to sell our house and belongings in a hurry. That made it so easy for all of us, a gift from the Lord.

We had arranged to spend most of our summer visit in CZ splitting our time between Prague and Písek. We had many friends in Prague, felt connected to the church in Vinohrady, and, of course, planned to help them with English Camp again that summer. We also looked forward to reconnecting with Miriam, Jírka, and Ondřej in Písek and hoped to meet more people and begin to get established there.

We were still in Prague at the start of our visit when we got a phone call from home. Shannon was in the hospital with an attack of acute pancreatitis. But how could this be? I thought the Lord said he was going to remove illness from among us. I apparently assumed we would have no more major illnesses in our family, only normal, less critical health problems. I didn't understand at first, but then the obvious occurred to me — you can't remove what isn't there. In other words, if there is no illness present, there is no illness to remove. We prayed that the Lord would remove that illness from Shannon and he did, so rather than having to return home to help, we were free to go on to Písek.

We wanted to spend two separate weeks in Písek that summer and had asked Miriam to let people from the church know when we would be in town in case anyone wanted to meet us. The first visit was in June and it was cold. Cold enough, at least, that someone was burning coal to heat their home. I had hoped for better air and weather in the summer. I was a bit discouraged because the fumes burned my lungs as we walked to the Cirkev Bratrská church on Tyršova that first Sunday morning.

At the beginning of the service Ondřej introduced Roy and me to the church and announced that we would be there all week and would like to meet with anyone who would like to meet us. Then Ondřej preached about following Jesus. He read from the Bible and parts of these verses struck me, "Jesus said, ... 'Very truly I tell you, ... when you are old you will stretch out your hands, and someone else will ... lead you where you do not want to go. (...) Follow me!'" (John 21:17-19) It sounds harsh, doesn't it? But it wasn't at all. I knew the Lord was speaking very gently and specifically to me, knowing I was beginning to waver about moving because I was concerned about Shannon and my weak lungs and the difficult air. He was making it clear that I just needed to follow him, no matter what. He wasn't demanding. He was comforting and encouraging as he acknowledged that he knew and understood my thoughts and fears and was taking all that into consideration as he continued to guide us to move to Písek.

That evening we had a pleasant meal with Jírka and Miriam, who were expecting their first child very shortly. It was really nice to be with them again and share in their excitement. Jírka was learning English at work and Miriam spoke it well because she had been to the U.S. for two extensive, work-related visits. We also appreciated the connection we shared with Miriam because she used to live in Prague, had gone to the English Camp, and knew the same people.

The next day we enjoyed a visit with Ondřej and meeting his wife, Tereza, who welcomed us with infectious enthusiasm. She bustled about the kitchen preparing a meal while chatting and laughing with us. Ondřej had an interactive kind of humor that felt like improvisational theatre, complete with sound effects, transporting us to imaginary scenes where we were participants. He would make me laugh 'til my sides hurt.

Of course, there were serious moments, too. With a twinkle in his eye, Ondřej mentioned that he did a "background check" on us and looked up our church in Virginia. We commended him for that and agreed it was wise because the Bible warns Christians to be discerning and to beware of "wolves in sheep's clothing" who come into churches to try to destroy them. Ondřej had concluded that Reston Bible Church was legitimate, healthy, and safe.

We went on to discuss our ministry plans. Roy and I had been thinking we could offer English lessons to adults who had fewer opportunities to learn English. But Ondřej had wanted us to do a week-long English Camp for young people every summer, like the camps he used to go to. That's all? We were so confused. Why did the Lord want us to quit our jobs and move to Písek just to do a camp one week a year?

Ondřej's experience with English Camps was that an American team did everything, what some Czechs call the "all-inclusive plan" or "camp-in-a-box". It includes choosing a theme for the week, writing and printing a camp book, preparing English lessons, songs, skits, T-shirts, crafts, and telling personal life stories as part of an evening program. Ondřej thought we already had a team in America to do everything. We didn't. That kind of camp would be a lot easier to organize while living in the States rather than Písek.

Our experience with the Prague church had been very different. The Czech leaders did most of the camp preparations and we native English speakers only prepared English lessons and shared doing workshops and evening programs. The very idea of trying to organize a team to do everything gave us palpitations because it was completely foreign to our experience and natural abilities. Some of that had to do with our age. Were we supposed to come up with ideas for skits, games, and activities for teenagers? Really? How? We weren't very creative. But how could we resist Ondřej? He was so enthusiastic about doing an English Camp. Besides, he was the local pastor and knew the situation; we didn't. Roy and I thought there was no reason we couldn't at least start with a camp as Ondřej wanted. (Gulp!) But the three of us agreed that the students from the church would take on the leadership, as in Prague, and Roy and I would recruit a team of native English speakers to handle the teaching.

One final issue came up which was a bit vague. In spite of Ondřej's precautions and confidence in us, we sensed a little awkwardness when he said something about being the youngest in the church leadership. We got the impression that some of the people were not enthusiastic about a couple from America joining them. Uh oh. Nevertheless, Ondřej seemed cautiously optimistic about Roy and me joining with the church.

All of that happened the first couple days we were in town. And then we were alone the rest of that week. No one contacted us. We began to fear that we were right about our impression that the church was concerned about Roy and me joining them. Having nothing else to do we explored more of the forest, wandered the streets in town, and kept returning to Biograf for meals because it was a non-smoking restaurant, a rarity in those days. The food was great and it was nice getting to know Nouri, who waited on us every day. After about five days he asked us why we were still there. He said it wasn't typical for tourists to stay more than a few days. When we explained that we were moving to town, he was really excited. It was especially heartwarming since we weren't sure how welcome we were in general. We were grateful for encouragement from Nouri, who ironically wasn't from Písek, but Tunisia.

But I was struggling as I returned to Prague. Did we hear the Lord correctly, or was it our imagination? I needed to start all over and figure out if we were really supposed to move to Písek, or even to the Czech Republic at all.

We enjoyed our time in Prague, as we always did, and the following Sunday the pastor, Pavel, began by reading the Bible. And what did he happen to read? "Go from your country, your people ... to the land I will show you. ... and I will bless you." (Genesis 12:1-2 TNIV) I looked at Roy with eyes wide open and whispered, "No way!" Pavel didn't know what that verse meant to us. OK, I got it. We really were supposed to move to CZ, but maybe we were wrong about Písek.

We shared our confusion and concern about Písek with a friend in Prague who offered some insight. Apparently, a few years earlier the Písek church had a bad experience with an American missionary/pastor (not Bert) and the church was still healing from the wounds when we came on the scene. Oh, great. NOT what we needed. No wonder the people at the Písek church were concerned about more Americans coming. We understood how they must have felt.

Meanwhile, we were getting tempting invitations to serve in Prague. Roy was asked to help at the Czech Technical

University (CVUT), someone from an international school, Riverside School, asked us to work there, and there were many, many other opportunities offered through our growing network of Czech friends. My head was swimming as we spent another exciting and exhausting week at English Camp in the Krkonoše. I found myself praying that the Lord would PLEASE let us go to Prague instead of Písek.

It was again in church when the Lord spoke words of guidance to us. The guest preacher at the church in Vinohrady that Sunday read Jeremiah 6:16, "This is what the Lord says: 'Stand at the crossroads and look; ask for the ancient paths, ask where the good way is, and walk in it, and you will find rest for your souls." Roy and I couldn't miss the Lord's direction to follow his trail marker and stick to the original, "ancient" plan of moving to Písek.

OK we understood what we had to do, but we decided that we would at least cancel our second visit to Písek that summer. Miriam had given birth to a beautiful baby boy, so she was really busy, and we didn't want to put any unnecessary strain on Ondřej and Tereza. We decided to enjoy an extra week in Prague with friends. It also gave us time to make a site visit to a TEFL (Teaching English as a Foreign Language) program that had looked promising online.

As we walked to church the last Sunday before leaving for the U.S., I was thinking about the different ways the Lord had answered our prayers for guidance so clearly during this trip and how it had always been on Sundays at church. I couldn't imagine him doing that again that morning. It turned out I was mistaken. Pastor Pavel summed up his sermon with these words, "The bottom line is that you go where God tells you to go, when God tells you to go there." Amazing! Afterward we told Pavel how the Lord had spoken to us through what he said. A look of enlightenment crossed his face. "That explains it," he said. "I had prepared to speak on Genesis 19 and how Lot was warned to flee for safety, but when I started preaching the Lord told me he wanted me to give that specific direction about going where we're told, when we're told."

We couldn't miss all the trail markers and flew home at the end of the summer with no further doubt in our minds that we really were moving to Písek. I know what you must be thinking. "Oh sure. You've said that before." True. But that time my mental struggle really was over.

"Your Word is a lamp to my feet and a light for my path." (Psalm 119:105)

9

> "The truth is, of course, that what one regards as interruptions are precisely one's life."
> ~ C. S. Lewis

Shortly after we returned to the States, Ondřej mentioned in one of his emails that Kenosha Bible Church organized the English Camps he went to when he was younger. Kenosha Bible Church?! Could it be the same Kenosha Bible Church in Kenosha, Wisconsin near where I grew up in Illinois and where my family still lived? We were going there in a couple of weeks to visit family. I called the church and asked if they were indeed the church that organized English Camps with a church in Liberec, CZ. Yes, they were. I asked if we could meet with some of their team when we were in the area. Yes, we could. They invited us to join them for the church service on Sunday morning and to stay afterward for lunch. Perfect.

Ben and his Czech wife, Helena, sat with us at lunch. Imagine our surprise when Helena told us that she knew Ondřej from Liberec because they went to the same English Camp. During our conversation it was obvious that she was familiar with Ondřej's great sense of humor. That visit was such a fun trail marker. We so appreciated the encouragement of the church in Kenosha and the timing was good because we were about to encounter a new challenge.

The fact that we had been advised by our Czech friends not to join a mission agency was a problem for many in our church in Virginia, including a few members of the missions committee. That, in turn, was a problem for us because the Lord had been confirming to Roy and me that our Czech friends were right and we were to take a different path than to join an agency. God wanted us to simply live in Písek, join the local church, teach English, and tell anyone who was interested about the good things he had done for us. That was it.

The concerns of the missions committee were reasonable for most situations, but didn't fit ours. This is how we addressed their main concerns:

:: *How will you be kept spiritually accountable?*
We will be accountable the same way we are now: through direction in the Bible, God's leading, and fellowship with people in the local church. We previously lived overseas in two countries for a total of five years and continued our walk with the Lord there, just as we do in the U.S.

:: *What about financial support and accountability?*
Our desire is to be good stewards of the Lord's money. Roy has a modest pension that includes subsidized medical insurance for both of us. We believe the pension is enough for ordinary living costs so we can be self-supporting.

:: *How will you navigate the transition logistics?*
We are blessed to have many Czech friends who have already helped with forms, translation, "ground truth" about living there, searching for housing, etc., and have offered to help in any other way they can. All of this supplies what an agency might do for us and has the advantage of strengthening relationships as we and the Czech church help one another.

:: *How will you handle culture shock?*
Because of Roy's career, we had already lived overseas and dealt with culture shock. That was in addition to the time we spent in Kenya, where we first met. And we ourselves were surprised to find that, more than in any other country where we had lived, Czech culture had a familiar feeling, a feeling of being at home.

Eventually the whole committee was in agreement with us. We were given the official blessing of our church and that meant a lot.

Meanwhile, we had decided to postpone our move until after Christmas and New Years so we could spend the holidays with our family. And we had continued to make arrangements for our move. We gathered the documents required by the Czech Government for our visa: financial records, criminal background check, fingerprints, etc. Ondřej provided the official Letter of Invitation.

Miriam was helping us look for a flat as we searched online every day. It seemed every time we found a suitable place it was taken immediately, before Miriam had a chance to inquire. Eventually the best flat of all that we had seen became available in the building next to hers. Once again Miriam quickly contacted the owner and that time it was available. She made all the arrangements for us to rent it. It was perfect.

We booked the teacher training at TEFL Worldwide Prague, the same place we had visited over the summer. The two instructors, one from Oxford and one from Cambridge, offered an impressive combination of expertise and experience. We signed up to begin in January.

We hired a moving company so we could send some books and other personal belongings. And, of course, we booked our airline tickets. Everything was ready and we were going to be on our way shortly, or so I thought.

Two days before the movers were scheduled to come and pack up our things, I had an appointment with a dermatologist who found some skin cancer on my nose and sent me to a special surgeon. No problem, I thought. I would just have it taken out and be on my way. It's surprising how often I am wrong. The surgeon had to remove quite a bit of my nose and informed me that I was going nowhere for the next two months.

As we wrote to our friends, "The heart of man plans his way, but the Lord directs his steps." (Proverbs 16:9) How true.

To be honest, I ended up being quite happy that I was stuck in the U.S. as my nose healed because I had to cover it with a large white bandage, causing me to resemble a bird known as the American Coot. You can google it. It wasn't how I wanted to look when I was going to meet people in Písek. I was able to get rid of the bandage after a couple months, but by then I had complications from a skin graft so that by the time we finally did move to Písek I had a scar that looked like a piece of ham on my nose. Great.

10

> "Little by little, one travels far."
> ~ Anonymous

In March 2011 we finally became official residents of Písek. Our flat was not yet available so we stayed at Villa Conti again. Two significant things happened at church on our first Sunday. A man whom we hadn't met before welcomed us warmly. At first he tried to do that in Czech, as if he was sure we must understand his meaning simply because his words sprang from his very full heart. But the puzzled look on our faces must have finally communicated that it wasn't working because he stopped, smiled, opened wide his arms, and embraced both of us at the same time. That was a gesture we understood. We appreciated his bold move even more after we learned what a break from Czech culture that was. Americans are comfortable hugging each other, but Czechs are more comfortable shaking hands.

And after the church service, Miriam introduced us to another man, Mirek, who invited us for coffee that afternoon. What a pleasant surprise to be invited by someone else in the church. Conveniently, he and his family lived in a house behind the small complex of flats where we would be living, only a three minute walk away. Mirek and his wife, Halka, had lived in Australia for a few years before they had children, so they both spoke English and communication was easy. We immediately felt comfortable with them. Their two teenage daughters, Veronika and Elíska, were among the students who would be helping with the Písek English Camp.

It was during that first visit that Mirek made a confession to us. He admitted that when we visited Písek the previous summer, he sensed the Lord telling him to be our friend. But Mirek didn't want to, nor did he think he had time to be friends with strange Americans. Ha ha ha! We loved him for that. What an honest, transparent man who we could relate to so well because of our own shortcomings. Mirek and Roy became good friends and still are to this day. Halka also became a good friend. Mirek and Halka reminded me of my father and mother. My dad was a talented craftsman who made a career of building custom homes. My mother was the one who kept an eye on the financial side so that my creative dad could actually get paid for his work and earn a living. Mirek and Halka were similar. Mirek was a master craftsman who designed and, with the help of his crew, built custom interiors for residential and commercial spaces. Halka ran the office and kept the books. They were a good team. If we needed someone to organize something, Halka was the right woman for the job. That first Sunday we began to hope that maybe living in Písek was going to work out after all.

After a few days, Miriam's parents invited us to stay with them while we continued to wait to move into our flat. Ernest and Věra were very gracious hosts and we enjoyed being with them. Meals together were a time for Czech lessons. Věra would point to the table, "Stůl."

We repeated, "Stůl."

She pointed to a napkin, "Ubrousek."

In unison, "Ubrousek."

A knife, "Nůž."

"Nůž."

We went on like that all week. Obviously Věra was a patient woman.

Then we were off to Prague to meet an American friend who was in town for a week. At the end of her visit, I had to return to the States to finish laser treatments on my nose while Roy returned to Písek to move into our "tropical" flat with its colorful walls: mandarin orange, lemon yellow, and lime green. Upon my return on Easter weekend in April, Roy met me at the airport with a suspicious grin and ... what was that? A whip made out of braided willow branches and decorated with ribbons? He said it was called a *pomlázka* and the local custom required that he do his duty on Easter Monday and give me a bit of a whipping for good luck. "Ha ha! Very funny. Put that thing away."

I had returned just in time for the 4-week TEFL course, which we had rescheduled since we couldn't do it in January. In retrospect we were so glad that the Lord had redirected our steps because the timing of taking that course in the spring, when we had more energy, rather than the dead of winter, was a blessing. The website described their particular course as being "intensive". That was honest advertising. On the second night we were up until 3:00 a.m. doing homework. The pace eased somewhat as we became more proficient, but it was a constant challenge to keep up, especially because we were among the few older students in a class of mostly 20-somethings. We were grateful, however, for the excellent teachers and all the valuable, practical lessons they packed into a very short amount of time. It was with a real sense of gratitude and accomplishment that we returned to Písek with TEFL Worldwide Prague certificates in hand. Hooray!

11

"A simple 'hello' could lead to a million things."
~ Anonymous

Back in Písek we were beginning to get desperate. Although we began the previous November trying to recruit native English-speaking volunteers for camp, it was now mid-May and we only had one. By then most Americans, who typically only have two weeks vacation time each year, had already locked in their summer plans. I got a knot in my stomach every time I saw the posters in town advertising our English Camp with a "team" from America. The first day of camp on 7 August was coming fast. It wasn't that our American friends weren't interested in helping. They were. It was just that some had time, but no money for airline tickets, while others had money, but no time to get away. We finally remembered a friend's kind offer of financial help if we ever needed it. That was it! We would ask him to buy airline tickets for volunteers who needed the help. The Lord had organized his people to work together solving the time and money issue so we ended up with our dream team of volunteers.

With that burden off our shoulders, why not take a break? My niece, Jane, was getting married in June and since we couldn't go to the wedding, I offered to meet the newlyweds on their honeymoon. Seriously! They were going on an Adriatic cruise and one of the ship's ports-of-call was Koper, Slovenia, just a six-hour drive from Písek. Perfect. They actually agreed to our plan! In the middle of our few, delightful days in Koper, the gigantic ship anchored, and Jane and her new husband, Matt, disembarked. We enjoyed a nice lunch together before wishing the happy couple *bon voyage.*

Meanwhile, our flat was still empty except for a mattress on the floor and a small wooden bistro set. At the same time that we were busy preparing for both the Prague and Písek English Camps, we were also making trips to IKEA trying to figure out how to best furnish our flat. Some people like doing interior decorating, but I don't because I find making those kinds of decisions a bit stressful. I like too many of the little showrooms in IKEA. I just wanted our new home to feel inviting and comfortable, a cheerful place where people would feel welcome and want to come to visit. In the interest of being efficient and paying for only one delivery, we had to "bite the bullet", make a decision about all the furniture for the whole flat, and buy it all at the same time. Delivery day came and the men filled our main room with a huge pile of boxes. Bert was in town visiting and helped assemble some of it, as did a couple guys from church, but we were still knee-deep in boxes when the American team arrived.

Camp in August was really great! You would never know that those students from the Písek church were hosting an English Camp for the first time. The leadership was as talented and loving as the Prague group. They had a lot of creativity and did a spectacular job, with a good balance of work and fun, silliness and serious discussions. Some adults from the church came to help and it was good to have time together to get to know each other a little bit. It was an encouragement to begin to feel accepted and to enjoy each other. We were grateful that Ondřej had persuaded us to do the camp that we hadn't really wanted to do at first. It was an unexpected blessing.

Another happy result of camp was that two of our American volunteers first met each other there and are now married. How sweet!

One day after camp we and one of our American volunteers were in Farmařske Potraviny, already one of our favorite local shops offering fresh, local food. Roy and he were discussing the merits of raw milk compared to pasteurized. Apparently the shop owner overheard us speaking English and must have recognized Roy and me. She slipped out from behind the counter and, while the guys were lost in their conversation, came up to me and said, "I can teach you Czech, if you want."

Have you ever had an experience when you meet someone for the first time and feel an instant connection? That is just how I felt. She introduced herself as Markéta and went on to describe her credentials and experience, which were very impressive. Yes, of course we would like to have her teach us. As helpful as stůl, ubrousek, nůž, etc were, we knew we needed more. She gave me her contact information and we agreed to start sometime in September.

I was amused as Markéta joined the guys and settled the matter with a scientific explanation, in English, of why it was important to pasteurize milk for food safety. They were caught off-guard — but impressed.

As we left the shop, I told Roy that we were going to be taking Czech lessons from the shop owner. We didn't know it then, but it was the beginning of a very special relationship with Markéta and her family.

12

"The ornament of a house is the friends who frequent it."
~ Ralph Waldo Emerson

With the camps behind us we began to settle down and feel more at home in our adopted town. The air was better than I experienced during our first visits. We figured out grocery shopping at Albert's and other shops. At church, Ondřej was a really good teacher of the Bible as well as a wise, caring pastor. He would email a copy of his sermon in Czech to us and we would plug it into Google translate, print it, and read along as he taught. It was actually a good exercise for helping us to learn Czech. We continued to have coffee on most Sunday afternoons with Mirek and Halka and those were special times together. Other people at the church welcomed us warmly. And we began our Czech lessons with Markéta.

Markéta was a great teacher and I feel bad that I wasn't a better student. However, I learned enough Czech to communicate around town, or at least I thought I did. Many times my Czech must have provided confusion or amusement for those with whom I tried to talk and I sometimes wondered what people thought after an encounter with "the American lady". For example, after only a couple months of Czech lessons I told a lady at the bank that the police wanted to talk to her. *"Co?!"* (What?!) She looked alarmed. I nodded as I smiled encouragingly because I thought I was thanking her for giving me a bank document for the foreign police so I could renew my visa.

I remember being in Emil Gaigher's Bakery one busy morning when the line of customers was up the stairs and almost out the door to the street. Although some people were talking quietly to each other as they waited, when it was our turn everyone stopped their conversations abruptly, causing a pronounced silence. In spite of suddenly becoming the awkward center of attention, Roy must have done OK because he actually got what he thought he ordered and on our way out another customer smiled at him in seeming approval.

The most stressful shopping we did was at Markéta's shop. We always wanted to do a good job speaking to her or her employees so we wouldn't embarrass her. One day Markéta wasn't there and we noticed a new, male shop assistant who looked a lot like her. Before leaving I took a deep breath and ventured to ask, *"Pardon. Markéta tatínek?"* He smiled and nodded. At the next Czech lesson I learned I should have used *otec* (father) because *tatínek* (daddy) was too familiar. Oooops. And yes, her father, Eda, was helping out at the shop as he was retired and, according to Markéta, had lots of free time.

In the autumn of 2011 we also began to offer a variety of English activities. We met individually with some teenagers from camp and the church who wanted to practice the English they were learning in school.

I began teaching English lessons in our flat to adults whom Roy and I met around town, as well as to people from the church and their friends. For two years before moving to Písek, I taught entry-level English through a program at our church. My class included students from Iran, Iraq, Afghanistan, Kyrgyzstan, Bulgaria, Portugal, Vietnam, and El Salvador. Those students were really great but I have to say that teaching Czech students who all spoke the same first language and used basically the same alphabet as English was much easier. I enjoyed them so much that my classes felt more like hosting a party.

Roy taught a class in our flat and also held conversational English meetings at local cafes. Later, Nouri helped Roy get permission to use a meeting room at the Biograf for his conversation groups, which was convenient for everyone.

We thought about charging a fee for our lessons and donating the money back to the town, but when we learned how complicated it would be to fulfill all the legal and accounting requirements, we decided to volunteer instead. However, we tried to be very careful not to compete with Czech teachers of English, so we only accepted students who otherwise would not have chosen to take lessons. We expected students to buy their own books and we asked that they contribute tea and snacks for the group classes, which they were happy to do.

We noticed that a couple of teens lived upstairs from us and I wanted to offer to meet with them so they could practice English, just as we were doing with the other teenagers, but I thought I should wait until I learned more Czech before attempting an invitation. After about six months, I ran into one of them in the stairwell and tried to communicate the offer. He patiently listened to me struggle along with my very limited Czech until finally, in perfect English, he said, "You can speak English, if you want." After I got over the shock, I laughed as I was able to much more clearly invite him, Jírka, and his sister, Aneta. Eventually we formed a club with all the teenagers instead of meeting with them individually. It was a lot more fun as they could play English games together and it was a much more efficient use of our time.

Over the next two years our classes and groups continued to grow as we and our students invited their friends and family. Markéta joined Roy's conversation group and she invited her parents, Eda and Hana, to join our other classes. I invited my hairdresser, Eliška, who invited her niece, Adél. Tereza, our pastor's wife, invited her friend, Alena, who invited her partner's brother, Vlad'a. Eva, from church invited her colleague, Járka, who invited her friend's daughter, Julie. Daniela and Jana each invited a colleague from work. Our neighbor, Marcela, whom we had never met, wondered what was going on in our flat and asked some students as they were leaving one day after class. She ended up joining my class and inviting Libor, who, as of this writing, is still doing lessons with us over Skype.

One invitation even resulted in our being able to help a local English teacher. Lucie, in Roy's conversation group, invited her English teacher, Iva, who asked Roy if he would come to her school once a week so her students could practice conversing with a native English speaker. Her plan was to rotate through all five of her classes so that each week Roy met with a different group of students until they all had a turn, and then begin the cycle again. It was perfect because rather than interfering with Iva's business, Roy was actually able to help her with it. It was during one of those sessions at Iva's school, across the street from the church, that the students asked Roy why we were in Písek, as you read in the opening of this story.

Our church on Tyršova was working together with the Elim Church that Bert had been part of. Remember Bert, the Dutch-American who lived in Písek for seven years? Well, a young couple from that church asked Roy and me to help their church find a mature American couple to join them as Bert and his wife had done before and as Roy and I were doing at our church. We told them we would be glad to help with their search.

Life in Písek was good. We enjoyed our students and hoped they learned as much from us as we learned from them. I had no idea I would enjoy teaching English so much. I found it much more difficult to be a student, but learning Czech was just as rewarding. Not only was Markéta a great teacher, she became a very dear friend, as did her family. What a gift to learn enough Czech to be able to function better around town! It made life in Písek much richer.

Eventually we learned enough Czech to make our annual trip to the foreign police to renew our visas without the help of a translator. The officer shook her head as she took my photo out of the processor. Showing it to me, she offered, *"Ještě?"* I have never been photogenic and I was thankful for another chance. But the next two or three attempts were no better. Finally, I gave up and made use of a phrase from my Czech course book, *"Nejsem žádná modelka."* (I am not a model.) The officer laughed and processed my visa.

Our friendships were growing deeper and no longer were all the faces around town strangers to me. If Písek was a family, we felt like the pet dog. We knew we would never belong in the same way a family member does, but we still felt at home and that was a blessing.

We enjoyed the town, too. It was a thriving place that offered so much in the way of culture, history, nature, restaurants, shops and more — all within walking distance. It was a town where ancient architecture and traditions blended with contemporary. A town that used its name Písek, which means "sand", as inspiration for an annual sand sculpture festival. A town that some Czechs affectionately called "Little Prague".

Yes, life in the beautiful, bustling town of Písek was good!

13

> "Our Father refreshes us on the journey
> with some pleasant inns,
> but will not encourage us
> to mistake them for home."
> ~ C.S. Lewis

One January evening in 2013, we got a call from our son, Scott. His four-year-old daughter, Lucy, was in the hospital with severe pneumonia. Lucy was born with a rare, primary immune deficiency called Hyper-IgE, or Job's Syndrome, which causes vulnerability to skin and lung infections, weak joints, etc.

I was terrified as I prayed for her healing, admittedly with very little faith. Early the next morning, just as Roy was beginning to wake up, he had a vision or half-waking dream. He saw Lucy and she was with Jesus, not that Roy saw Jesus, he was just aware of Lucy being with someone, a vague silhouette of a person that Roy somehow knew was Jesus. Lucy was happy and excited as she said, "Look, Granddad! I can JUMP!" Jumping was significant because Lucy's weak joints prevented her from even being able to hop, which used to upset her very much because she was unable to do what the other children in her preschool could do. "Can you hop?" was a question she often asked of people. So a vision of Lucy being able to jump was amazing.

An incoming phone call woke Roy up completely. It was Scott and he was in tears because his little girl was dying. He said she was cold and gray and her oxygen levels were dangerously low. The hospital staff had arrived with the bereavement cart full of tissues and other items for him and his wife, Jan.

Breathtaking heartache! How did Lucy's dying match up with removing illness from among us, as I thought the Lord showed me before we moved? I didn't understand. We notified our friends at church and asked them to pray, and a team of four women especially focused on it. I began packing as Roy got online to book our flight home.

About an hour later, Scott called again and said the doctors told them not to give up hope because Lucy was suddenly doing better and might survive. Really?! Wow! Thank you, Lord! We were cautiously optimistic, but we still packed funeral clothes before flying back to the U.S.

Lucy was put on a ventilator and continued to improve. After coming off of it two weeks later, she very gradually regained her strength. In spite of being oxygen-deprived for so long, Lucy did not suffer any brain or organ damage. It was an absolutely amazing answer to prayers! God did the impossible and removed even that illness from among us when he spared Lucy. He answered the prayers of the team of four beyond our wildest dreams. How thankful we were!

It was with grateful hearts that we returned to Písek in February after Lucy's recovery and picked up where we left off with our Czech lessons and English classes. It felt good to be back.

That spring Scott finished his residency at Georgetown Hospital in Washington, DC and accepted a job offer with an anesthesiology group in Richmond, Virginia, which was two hours south of our home in Reston. Roy and I had to return to the U.S. that summer to decide what to do with our house. At first we planned to rent it out, but in the end we decided to sell it. First we had to get rid of everything inside, which was no small job. We ended up giving away most of of our furniture, selling a few things, and storing some photos and heirlooms in a 2x2 meter storage unit. By the time we returned to Písek in August we felt wonderfully free — no cars, no house, not much "stuff".

As we began our third year of teaching in Písek in the autumn of 2013, our network of contacts had grown to include Veronika, who was related to Martina in Roy's conversation group. Veronika and her husband owned a small farm complex in the tiny village of Jarotice, not far from Písek. Their property included a guest house that could comfortably accommodate about twelve people, with more accommodation in other buildings on the farm. They had worked very hard to nicely renovate everything with the idea of hosting small groups.

I had an idea! We could do weekend retreats with our students. We booked three consecutive weekends in May 2014 to make sure we had enough flexibility and availability so each of our students could come. All of our students signed up for one of the weekends and everyone was looking forward to it as we began planning activities together. Roy and I thought we might also have a chance to answer the "why are you here" question in more depth around a campfire.

Then we went home for Christmas where, to our surprise and dismay, we faced another crisis. Our daughter, Shannon, was suffering from complications of Lyme disease (borreliosis). Lyme disease seemed to aggravate Shannon's pancreatic condition. But her bigger problem was that her marriage was failing, causing her a lot of stress which also aggravated her weakened pancreas. The combination was too much for her and her young children. We knew we needed to move back to the U.S. to be near them in Pennsylvania so we could support them. It was heartbreaking to see them suffer so.

With heavy hearts we returned to Písek long enough to meet with each of our classes and groups to tell them the disappointing news that we were leaving for an indefinite period of time. We kept our flat in the hope of being able to return in the summer, but we still had to cancel the planned weekend retreats because of the uncertainty.

Staring blankly out the airplane window on the way back home, my mind was a jumble of memories, questions, concerns, prayers. I remembered another question Czechs asked us almost as often as why we were there. "How long are you staying?" We didn't know, but we hoped it would be a long time. The Lord showed us to move to Písek and we knew some day he would show us when it was time to return home. Privately Roy and I had loosely planned on ten years, but was this the beginning of the end?

Only a few months earlier we had gotten rid of all our furniture and other household items in Virginia, assuming we'd live in Písek many more years. Now in February we were moving into a short-term rental flat in Pennsylvania with only an air mattress to sleep on and a small folding table with four folding chairs, just as we had started out with in our Písek flat. At least it was an easy move with so little furniture. Shannon loaned us some dishes and we picked up a few groceries just before a big snowstorm hit and we couldn't go anywhere for a few days. Within a couple weeks we were visited by Liz, a woman who lived nearby and had volunteered at the same English Camp we had, which was hosted by the Prague church. She and one of the Czech leaders had fallen in love and she was in the process of moving there to eventually marry him. Would we like to borrow her furniture? Why, yes we would, thank you very much! God's unique provision — again. Perfect!

At first we thought Shannon and her children would only need us for a few months and then Roy and I would return to Písek. We kept extending the lease on our flat a few months at a time and made a brief visit in January 2015. But in the summer of 2015, our landlady got a better offer from someone who could pay more and commit to a two-year lease. He even wanted our flat furnished just the way it was so the landlady offered to buy most of our furniture, which made that part of our moving much easier. It was through these clear trail markers from the Lord that we knew our move back to the US was more permanent.

In addition, quite independent of Roy and me, our church found another church in the US to partner with for English Camps and the Elim Church found the mature couple they were looking for. We never met the family, but we were encouraged by the Lord's provision in answers to prayers for both churches.

The process of deciding to move back home was nothing like the process I went through when deciding to move to Písek. Our family need was obvious and didn't require as much special revelation from the Lord about where to live, so I wasn't plagued with as many doubts about that.

We could see that Shannon's strength was failing under the heavy physical and emotional load she was carrying. Neither Roy nor I came from a broken home so we were unprepared for dealing with what Shannon and her children were going through with the break-up of their family. We made a lot of mistakes, especially at the beginning. I will spare you the details and spare myself the painful recollection. I felt like a hurting, frightened child but the Lord was a faithful friend and wise guide as he walked with us through that dark valley.

The process of deciding to move back home may have been straightforward, but the process of conquering my fear about the future of my daughter and grandchildren was not. That required much more from the Lord but I will only note his first specific communication to me on that subject.

February 10, 2014
"Fear not …
I will pour water on the thirsty land,
    and streams on the dry ground;
I will pour my Spirit upon your offspring,
    and my blessing on your descendants." (Isaiah 44:2-3)

God, as a loving Father, kept reassuring me that everything was going to be OK and that some day Shannon and the children would emerge from their trauma even stronger.

Over the years God has taught me a lot about himself and his power, wisdom, and love. He has also taught me something of what people suffer in these situations that I couldn't possibly have learned in any other way than to experience them first hand. And, to use a word picture, each time he burned off a little more of my dross. Just as gold or silver is refined by fire to remove impurities, or dross, so the Lord allows his children to go through fiery trials for the same ultimate good. "… when you walk through the fire, you shall not be burned, and the flame shall not consume you. For I am the LORD your God … (…)

… you are precious in my eyes, and honored, and I love you … Fear not, for I am with you …" (Isaiah 43:2-5)

On the one hand, there have been painful experiences that I would have avoided, if at all possible. On the other hand, I am grateful for all I learned and the precious treasures that I acquired along the way: more wisdom, strength, courage, faith, love, understanding, joy, freedom. Nothing can ever take those gifts from me.

In the Bible I had read many times over the years about how we must walk by faith, trusting God, and not just by physical sight, by what we see around us. We never have all the information we think we have. Or, as the saying goes, "We don't know what we don't know." Walking by faith always sounded so simple until each time I had to do it. I made progress that day in the hospital when I was sitting and praying at Scott's bedside as he appeared to be dying, and I was asking the Lord to heal him while at the same time releasing my emotional grip and putting him in God's hands. I made progress when I obeyed God's leading to move to Písek. I made more progress trusting him when Lucy nearly died. And I have been making even more progress trusting him to heal Shannon and her children from the trauma they have been going through. I am becoming stronger, freer, and even closer to the Lord than ever before. I imagine the lessons, training, and refining will continue until the day I die, but so will the sweet fellowship as I walk with the Lord.

14

> "Pravda vítězí."
> "Truth prevails."
> ~ Jan (John) Hus

How did a relationship between God and me begin anyway, especially since I didn't grow up in a Christian home?

It's surprising how seemingly insignificant events can sometimes change the course of our lives. That's just what happened when, as a high school student, I went to the movies with my family to see *MASH*, a satirical anti-war film set in a military field hospital during the Korean War. I was attracted to the excitement and camaraderie of the emergency medical team as they were able to save lives and help others. That led me to pursue a career in the medical field. I didn't want the responsibility of being a trauma doctor, though, so I decided to become a nurse because I thought it would be less stressful.

Naturally, while in nurses' training I saw a lot of people suffer and some die. That started to trouble me and I became cynical about life. I wondered why on earth we were born just to die. It seemed like a cruel joke. It didn't matter if I was good or bad, happy or sad, rich or poor, healthy or sickly, had a long or short life; at the end there was a box with my name on it. And then what? That question haunted me no matter how I tried to put it out of my mind.

I thought back to the summer when I was six years old. A local church hosted Vacation Bible School, a children's program teaching Bible stories, doing crafts, organizing outdoor activities, and providing snacks. All the kids in my neighborhood went. I'm sure our moms welcomed the opportunity to get free child care for a week. One day when it was time to go outside and play, the leaders asked who wanted to know how to go to heaven. Nobody raised their hand for the obvious reason that we all wanted to go outside and play. As the oldest in the group, the responsibility to volunteer fell to me, as it so often did. I resigned myself to my role and reluctantly raised my hand as all the other children raced out the door. I don't remember what the leaders told me, but I do remember thinking that going to heaven was so great that as soon as I got back to my neighborhood, instead of going straight home, I went around knocking on doors to tell people the amazing news. However, even at the tender age of six I could tell that I was being patronized and nobody was really interested, so I gave up and went home.

As I grew older I heard lots of theories about what would happen to me after I died: nothingness, reincarnation, nirvana, heaven/hell, etc. None of them could be proven. They all required faith. Believing God exists required faith; believing there was no God required faith. Believing in heaven required faith; believing in nothingness required faith. Was there any evidence that pointed to the truth?

I began looking for answers but I was afraid of being tricked into believing something that wasn't true, so I started to explore the various theories with a healthy amount of skepticism. If God was real, I couldn't believe that he existed in little statues made by people, so I crossed that off my list immediately. I briefly checked out the Ba'hai faith. Even though the grounds and temple nearby were beautiful and created a peaceful atmosphere, everything about the beliefs seemed too "airy fairy" — they didn't "ring true" or connect to real life. I attended a few meetings of a so-called Christian group but I didn't like the pressure tactics they used to try to control me. I later learned that the group was a counterfeit, a cult. I explored other religions that had various checklists of do's and don'ts to qualify for whatever their version of "heaven" was, but none of them was able to confirm how much was enough. How much good did I have to do to make up for the bad I had done? Nobody knew. I narrowed my search down to believing it was either Biblical Christianity or nothing.

My journey took me to a week-long Christian missions conference on a college campus in western Pennsylvania. One day a few of us went to the ice cream shop in the small town. As I was enjoying my strawberry sundae, one of the guys started saying something positive about Christianity. Without warning I lost my mind and exploded at the poor guy, accusing him and all Christians of not knowing how to have fun. Even as the words were escaping my mouth, my heart was condemning my own hypocrisy. I knew that deep down I felt anxious and hollow inside and neither the good things I did nor the pleasure I indulged in helped. I wasn't like that guy, who seemed to have a powerful peace and genuine joy about him. Later, when I wanted to apologize, I couldn't find him. Understandably, I think he avoided me from that time on, and since there were hundreds of people on the college campus for the conference, it was easy for him to do. I still blush as I remember how obnoxious I was.

The next day some friends invited me to skip the conference and go with them to check out a Christian music festival nearby, an annual event with thousands of people camping in a huge field for a few days. My friends and I all split up and agreed to meet at the car some hours later. As I wandered around alone, I remember feeling incredibly uncomfortable, like a fish out of water. I was not a Christian and I didn't belong. Christian musicians were performing; speakers were teaching from the Bible; people were praying, singing, talking, hanging out, cooking, eating, laughing, sleeping. And then I noticed some people waiting in line to be baptized by a man standing in a muddy pond.

To this day I can't explain why I got in that line. Baptism was for new Christians and I wasn't one, but I didn't know that at the time. When it was my turn, I stopped the man before he dunked me under water, which would symbolize the death of my old self, and raised me out of the water, symbolizing my new birth into eternal life with Christ. Not knowing any of that, I thought I could make up my own meaning, so I told the man to wait while I told him what I was doing by being baptized. I pointed in one direction as I said, "I used to go that way, away from God," and then turning and pointing in the opposite direction I continued, "but now I am going to go that way and go with God." The man said, "That's what baptism is," and dunked me.

I shrugged as I got out of the water. Was that all? Apparently my journey to find the truth about God and life and death was to be continued. But that night back at the dorm, as I was drifting off to sleep, something changed inside of me as I unexpectedly was filled with a deep sense of peace. It's hard to describe but something beautiful happened to me! I didn't know it then, but it was the Lord's loving touch and, to use one of Jesus' word pictures, I was "born again". He filled that nagging, gnawing emptiness inside of me with his very life, his Spirit.

God was so generous and kind to have accepted my small, ignorant, half-hearted bit of faith in deciding to "turn around" and follow him.

"Therefore, if anyone is in Christ, he is a new creation. The old has passed away; behold, the new has come." (2 Corinthians 5:17)

Ultimately, to my great surprise and joy, I discovered that there was strong evidence that God was real and the Bible was true. It was so compelling that it would have taken more faith for me to reject it as false than to trust it as true. There is no other book like it in all of history or in all the world, and it is still the most widely read book of all time. No other religious book made itself more vulnerable to higher criticism than the Bible as it incorporated history, geography, culture, specific names of people and places, detailed prophecy (most of which has already been specifically fulfilled), and even some science. It was as if God was begging us to challenge it, which many have done without honestly being able to refute its claims. The verifiable things in Scripture made it easier for me to trust the spiritual things which can't be verified in the same way. And although some spiritual things go beyond my reasoning, nothing goes against my reasoning. Therefore, it was reasonable for me to trust what the Bible says about life and death, heaven and hell, and what will happen to me after I die.

"Jesus said ..., 'I am the resurrection and the life. Anyone who believes in me will live, even though they die; and whoever lives by believing in me will never die. Do you believe this?'" (John 11:25-26)

Yes, I do.

My logic caught up with my experience, my mind with my heart. If my intellect had not been adequately satisfied, I never would have been willing or able to hold on to my faith as it has been attacked over the decades. If I had only dry facts of theology, but no tangible experience of Jesus' life in me, that wouldn't be enough either. I need both personal experience and compelling evidence.

And so it happened that at the age of twenty I was born again and became a follower of Jesus, the Messiah, and it is the best thing that has ever happened to me.

15

*"You have not chosen one another,
but I have chosen you for one another."*
~ C.S. Lewis

Because Roy and I spent so much time with younger Czechs, the topic of marriage, specifically our marriage, often came up. And since it is one of the good things God has done for me, I would like to tell you the story of how he brought it about.

Please return with me to the missions conference at the college campus in Pennsylvania where I had just become a Christian. The organization that hosted the conference also offered a scholarship to eight college students to spend the following summer doing missionary service somewhere in the world, yet to be determined. Even though I had been a Christian for only a couple days, I decided to apply. Never mind that I knew ... NOTHING. I just thought Jesus' gift was the most amazing, wonderful thing and everyone would want to know about it.

It turned out that not everybody was excited to hear the good news, as I discovered when I returned to my parents' home in northern Illinois. I should have remembered my experience when I was six years old and knocking on doors

But this time it was my family who were not excited. In fact, they were quite alarmed and assured me not to worry, that I would get over it. I reassured them that I wasn't crazy as I headed to my new home in Champaign-Urbana, about two hours south of Chicago. I was starting my first professional job as a nurse in the regional trauma center. Every hospital in Illinois had its own emergency room and within every 30-mile radius one of those hospitals was designated a regional trauma center. The town was the home of the University of Illinois with, at that time, 35,000 students and was surrounded by miles and miles of farmland. Our trauma center saw everything from farm accidents to what some reckless, "invincible" college students bring on themselves. It was a busy place but I loved my job.

I found a wonderful church. The pastor was a mature believer but the rest of us were new to the faith. Many were graduate students and some had come from a Jewish background and realized that Jesus is the Messiah, so we celebrated the Passover as well as Jesus' resurrection. I moved into a house with seven other young women from the church. We all were new believers and had a great time living and learning together. Those early days of being a Christian were like a very happy childhood. They were precious days with the Lord and my new Christian friends.

After work one day I found a letter waiting for me. I had been accepted for the missionary service program! Even though it had only been a few months since I became a Christian, I had already learned enough to know that I didn't know enough. Only one in one hundred applicants got accepted and I was one of them? What were they thinking? The letter also informed me that I would be going to Nairobi, Kenya. Cool!

The following June my parents took me to the airport to fly to Pennsylvania where, for the first time, I met the seven other members of our team the day before our flight to Kenya. It was my first international trip and I was excited!

Upon our arrival in Kenya, and before we began our work, the American missionary pastor who hosted our group arranged for us to recover from jet lag by going on a safari for a couple days. The original plan was for his wife to join us but she wasn't able to, so he invited an American guy named Roy to take her place. I was tired of meeting new people, so after greeting him politely I found a seat in the back of the van where I could take a break from making small talk with strangers.

Roy was a graduate student at Yale and had been in Nairobi for a year on a Rockefeller Foundation grant to do research for his PhD in development economics. Apparently Roy took a liking to me, but I was not interested in him or any other guy because I had been burned by a previous relationship. In fact, one of the many reasons I had been looking forward to the trip to Kenya was precisely to get away from those kinds of entanglements. I was pursuing my new dream of remaining single and having a fulfilling career in nursing.

Our team was divided into three groups and we rotated among three different projects: living in a Maasai village where we helped to build a dam; living in a village in the north of the country where we helped to paint a hospital; and staying in Nairobi with the pastor's family where we worked with children in a nearby slum.

Between each project we regrouped at the pastor's house for a couple days and Roy always seemed to be around. He was eager. I politely tried to avoid him. He had been raised by Christian parents but had been ignoring God yet questioning what was true about him. He was attracted to our group and wanted to learn more about why our faith was so real. But he was also attracted to me. It was awkward.

After each group finished all three rotations it was time to return home. Roy asked to drive me to the airport while the other seven went in the van. I was disappointed, but said OK. To my relief, when it was time to say good-bye, Roy just said, "Bye," and that was it. Whew. I found my seat on the airplane and, to my own confusion, found myself missing Roy, but not in a romantic way.

Life had gone back to being as normal as life ever is for a trauma nurse. Once again, one day after work there was a letter waiting for me. This one was from Roy. He was very excited because he had experienced being born again as a Christian. I was really, really happy for him!

For three months we continued to correspond using a method rarely in practice these days; we wrote letters with pen and paper. Roy quickly finished his research and wrote that he would be returning to his home in Connecticut in November and then wanted to visit me in Illinois. I agreed, but knew I needed to be proactive. So when I met Roy at the airport in Chicago, after saying hello I handed him a brochure entitled "Christian Single Adulthood" and told him that was my plan. With that issue settled, at least in my mind, we headed to my parents' house.

Even with my precaution, I was beginning to lose ground because my mom and dad really liked Roy. I saw my dad enjoying his company and my mom figured out his weakness for chocolate and made him her irresistible homemade fudge, ice cream sundaes with her homemade hot fudge sauce, and all sorts of other tempting treats. My little nine-year-old sister, Valerie, was my only ally. After I had gone to sleep one night, she went to Roy's room and asked him what his intentions were. Surprised by such a question from such a little kid, he wasn't sure how to answer. She went on to tell him that she just wanted him to know that I wasn't the "marrying kind". Ha ha!

A few days after Roy's arrival he and I drove to Ohio where my Kenya team was having a reunion. It was great fun to see everyone again and share all of our photos because, after all, in those days you couldn't see your photos until you dropped them off at a photo lab to be developed and then picked them up a week later in hard copy.

On our way back to Illinois, Roy wanted to visit one of his old college buddies in Indiana. While driving down the highway we were having an argument about marriage. Roy was defending its merits and I was pointing out its disadvantages.

Then Roy suddenly blurted out, "Will you marry me?"

And I answered, "Yes."

?!?!?!?!

I remember being shocked at my own answer.

"You will?" he asked, almost in disbelief.

Roy was getting excited; I was nervous and confused but kept telling myself that this guy was so determined at least he would be faithful.

We arrived at a Pizza Hut where we were meeting Roy's friend and his wife. Roy was bubbling over with excitement as he told them we were getting married. They asked how long we had known each other. We looked at each other and quickly calculated that we had spent a total of about two weeks together, mostly in a group setting. His friends looked worried, which frightened me, so I went to the ladies' room where I felt like I was going to be sick. Then, ever so subtly, I felt the Lord reassure me in unspoken words, telling me not to worry and that if Roy and I kept him first in our lives, he would bless our marriage.

Sometime shortly after our engagement my feelings caught up with my intellect. Good thing! Just as with my relationship with the Lord, I needed both my heart and mind to be in agreement in my marriage relationship. Roy is a good husband and I love him! The Lord has been the foundation that we have built our lives and marriage on. He has been faithful to bless us through all of our ups and downs over the past 45 years and we are grateful.

16

"A pleasure is not full grown until it is remembered."
~ C.S. Lewis

It may be obvious to you, dear reader, that I've never written anything like this before. Now I'm trying to figure out how to bring this little book to a close. Yes, I could go on and on writing about the good things God has done for me, but if I try that, I will never finish. For now I'll just tie up some loose ends.

Most of you already realize this, but the unusual story of how Roy and I got engaged and married should not serve as a pattern for anyone who is seeking to be married. I don't want to give false hope where affection is not reciprocal. Each couple has their own unique story. And if you are single don't assume that the "grass is greener" in married life. I believe both lifestyles have their special blessings and challenges.

Similarly, my story of how I became a Christian should not serve as a formula for anyone who is exploring. If you genuinely want to know if God is real and if what the Bible says is true, then I suggest asking God to somehow make himself known to you. He is very creative and will probably answer your request at a time you do not expect and in a way you do not expect, but in a way that will be unmistakable and special for you. He is the author of faith and your story will be uniquely yours. Reading the Bible and discussing your questions and concerns with Christians is also important when searching for answers. There are a few additional recommendations in the back of this book.

If you are a Christian you know that just as in any relationship, your relationship with God requires ongoing, open communication with him, mostly through reading the Bible and prayer, as well as being in fellowship with other believers.

If you are neither a Christian nor interested in exploring, then God has given you the freedom to choose and I respect your freedom.

What about our family? Looking back, I realized that God's timing was perfect in showing us when to return to the US because only he knew how much we were about to be needed. In addition to supporting Shannon and her children, Scott and his family needed us.

Lucy's condition, Job's syndrome, is so rare that only 1:1,000,000 people are born with it. After her dangerous encounter with pneumonia it was recommended that she become a patient of the US Government's National Institutes of Health (NIH). It is a medical research facility that studies and treats rare diseases because, in so doing, they make discoveries that help people with more common diseases.

Lucy's previous dangerous encounter with pneumonia permanently damaged an area in the lower lobe of her right lung which caused it to be more vulnerable to infection, especially given her compromised immune system. Her doctors suggested a bone marrow transplant which they hoped would benefit Lucy by replacing her deficient immune system with her mother's healthy one. The plan had its risks, including infection. Lucy would have to undergo chemotherapy to completely suppress her own immune system before she could receive the transplant from her mother. Even after receiving the transplanted immune system, it would take time before it could effectively protect Lucy from infection. The whole ordeal would keep Lucy at NIH for several months during which Roy and I would take care of her younger brother, Joel, in Virginia while Scott and Jan took turns staying with Lucy in Maryland.

The transplant took place on 11 December 2015 and the doctors periodically measured its progress. We were so grateful that test results kept showing good success. But in April, Lucy's new, improved immune system over-reacted as it attacked an infection which had developed around the damaged area in her right lung which, in turn, set off a dangerous inflammatory response. Ironically, at that point she needed steroids to calm down her new immune system.

Then one day Lucy's lung collapsed and she was moved to the ICU. After all she and her parents had been through, their hopes rising and falling, that was a devastating setback. The team of doctors had been agonizing about whether or not to do surgery to remove the infected, damaged lung tissue. Surgery was very high risk on someone with Job's disease and who also had just had a bone marrow transplant. Finally the decision was made for them when the bottom of Lucy's lung tore open and they had no choice but to operate. The bottom lobe of Lucy's right lung was removed, but within three days she was riding a tricycle down the hospital corridors! Once again the Lord healed Lucy. Amazing! That was in April of 2016, and how we celebrated as she was finally discharged! We were convinced that the worst was behind us and Lucy would never again have to face such trauma.

But we weren't finished, as the worst was yet to come for poor Little Lu. In December of that same year Lucy got pneumonia and had the same inflammatory over-reaction. Once again Scott and Jan were at the bedside of their dying little girl, who for the second time was given only a 10% chance of surviving. Once again Lucy was on a ventilator for two weeks. Once again the Lord kept Lucy alive. But that time after waking up she was unable to move anything except her toes. And because she was eight years old, she was old enough to be really scared that she would spend the rest of her life paralyzed. Lucy was very, very depressed. We all were.

And then, about two weeks later, Lucy shed tears of joy as she moved her hand. It was ever so slowly and ever so little, but there was no mistaking it, she could move her hand. Oh, thank you, Lord! It took quite some time for her to get her full strength back, but she did. Since then Lucy has been doing very well and is now 13 years old. Yes, she still has the underlying Job's syndrome, but we thank the Lord for what he has done so far.

By the way, Lucy's bone marrow transplant ordeal was filmed by the Discovery Channel for a documentary about research at NIH. Lucy was one of four patients they focused on to tell the story in a three-part series, *First In Human*.

Scott's health has remained fairly stable. Shannon is doing better, too, even though she is still physically weak. Her first marriage ended in divorce and since then she has remarried. Anyone who has been through the break-up of a family knows that some wounds take longer to heal than others, but the Lord has been gently working to heal Shannon and her two children who are now teenagers. Our eldest son, Craig, and his wife and four children don't have any unusual health or other issues and generally have been living less dramatic lives. Roy and I enjoy living in Pennsylvania near Shannon and her children, as well as being a reasonable drive away from our sons and their families in Virginia. Wonderful!

I would like to finish with a word to the people of Písek.

How grateful we are that the Lord gave us the gift of living in your town! It was a great idea and we never would have thought of it on our own. I'm thankful God was so patient and clear to lead us there as we stumbled along the path, looking for trail markers He didn't let us wander off and lose our way. Now that we are back in the States, we are thankful for opportunities to visit because our friendships haven't ended, they have only morphed into a new phase.

Now you know the real reason why we were in Písek. You, dear people, have been a wonderful part of the good things God has done for us as you have enriched our lives. Roy and I have very fond memories of our church family, dear friends, students, and neighbors. You invited us for meals, you gave us seasonal gifts from your gardens and goodies from your kitchens, you introduced us to local sights, activities, traditions, and so much more.

We also have good memories of those of you whose names we never knew: shop assistants, restaurant servers, bank clerks, the foreign police, medical staff, and some of you who just happened to observe us having trouble communicating and stepped in to help.

Písek will always have a special place in our hearts and we thank all of you for welcoming us and making our time of living there an incredible blessing.

Chapter Heading Citations

Chapter 1
J.R.R. Tolkien, *The Lord of the Rings: The Fellowship of the Ring.*

Chapter 2
C.S. Lewis, *The Complete C.S. Lewis Signature Classics, The Problem of Pain.*

Chapter 3
J.R.R. Tolkien, *The Hobbit.*

Chapter 4
The Hobbit: An Unexpected Journey, 2012 film. www.quotes.net/movies/the_hobbit%3A-an_unexpected_journey_146490.

Chapter 5
The Hobbit: An Unexpected Journey, 2012 film. www.quotes.net/movies/the_hobbit%3A-an_unexpected_journey_146490.

Chapter 6
J.R.R. Tolkien, *The Lord of the Rings: The Fellowship of the Ring.*

Chapter 7
J.R.R. Tolkien, *The Lord of the Rings: The Fellowship of the Ring.*

Chapter 8
C.S. Lewis, *Letters to Malcolm.*

Chapter 9
C.S. Lewis' letter to Arthur Greeves, cited in
The Collected Works of C.S. Lewis.

Chapter 10
This anonymous quotation is often misattributed to Tolkien, according to thetolkienist.com.

Chapter 11
Anonymous

Chapter 12
Ralph Waldo Emerson

Chapter 13
C.S. Lewis, *The Problem of Pain.*

Chapter 14
Jan (John) Hus, (c. 1372 - 1415), Czech reformer.

Chapter 15
C.S. Lewis, *The Four Loves.*

Chapter 16
C.S. Lewis, *Out of the Silent Planet.*

Additional Resources for Explorers

Keeping in mind that the Bible is the gold standard, the plumb line, the ultimate authority about the Christian faith, here are a few additional resources that might help the curious:

Mike Minter

As noted in my text, Roy and I attended Reston Bible Church. For nearly 25 years we sat under the excellent Bible teaching of Pastor Mike Minter. After 45 years of full-time ministry he recently became Pastor Emeritus. Videos of his sermons are available on the restonbible.org website.

Josh McDowell

As a bitter college student hostile against Christianity, McDowell wasn't as interested in discovering truth as he was in attacking the faith at its heart — the resurrection of Jesus. He correctly determined that the Christian faith would be worthless if Jesus didn't really rise from the dead. To his great surprise, the evidence for the resurrection was too compelling for him to reject. That was just the beginning of McDowell's comprehensive examination of evidence in response to questions and criticisms commonly raised about Christianity. For those who are curious about his findings:

:: *The New Evidence that Demands a Verdict*

"New" because it's an updated version of his earlier book on the same subject as even more evidence became available. The text is organized in a topical, encyclopedic format.

CS Lewis

Born in 1898 in Belfast, Ireland, Lewis earned two degrees from Oxford University: philosophy and English literature. He intended to teach philosophy but there were no openings, so instead he taught English literature at Oxford and later taught at Cambridge University. His journey from atheism to Christianity took place during his years on the faculty at Oxford. For those who are curious about the logical/philosophical credibility of Christianity:

:: *Mere Christianity*
A book that originated from radio talks that Lewis did for the BBC during WWII.

:: *CSLewisDoodle on YouTube*
Animated illustrations accompanied by readings from *Mere Christianity* and some of his other works.